Longman First Certificate
Read and Write

Roy Kingsbury and Guy Wellman

Longman Group UK Limited
Longman House, Burnt Mill, Harlow,
Essex CM20 2JE, England
and Associated Companies throughout
the world

© Longman Group UK Limited 1988
All rights reserved; no part of this
publication may be reproduced, stored in a
retrieval system, or transmitted in any
form or by any means, electronic,
mechanical, photocopying, recording, or
otherwise, without the prior written
permission of the Publishers.

First published 1988
ISBN 0 582 85285 4

Set in 9/10pt 'Monophoto' Plantin Light

Printed in Italy
by Milanostampa, Farigliano (CN)

Acknowledgements

We are grateful to the following for permission to reproduce copyright material:

The Editor, Bournemouth Evening Echo for cutting 'Underground route, not by rail' from *Bournemouth Evening Echo* 27.9.85; BP Petroleum Development Ltd for adapted extract and map from introduction to BP Green Leaflet *Wytch Farm Oilfield Developments: Purbeck to Southampton Pipeline*; Consumers' Association for article 'Getting Action on Complaints' pp 22–3 *Which?* Magazine Jan. '84; Mr Bernard Goss for an extract from his letter to *The Times* 4.12.86; Dr A.C. Klottrup, St. Chad's College, Durham for an extract from his letter to *The Times* 4.12.86; London Express News and Feature Services for article 'Drama of Double Crash' from *the Sunday Express* 25.11.84; Pan Books Ltd for an extract from *Funny Amusing and Funny Amazing* by Denys Parsons; Mrs E.W. Wakefield for an edited extract from her letter to *Bournemouth Evening Echo* 27.9.85; George Weidenfeld & Nicholson Ltd for item by Michael Noakes from *Robert Morley's Second Book of Bricks* by Robert Morley.

Photo acknowledgements

We are grateful to Barnabys Picture Library for permission to reproduce the photograph on page 35.

All other photographs by the Longman Photo Unit/Trevor Clifford

Illustrated by Jerry Collins, Hardlines, Donald Harley, Frances Lloyd, Liz Roberts, Chris Ryley and Stephen Wright.

Cover illustration by Andrew Aloof

Introduction
For Students and Teachers

Who this book is for

Read and Write has been specially written for students studying for the Cambridge First Certificate Examination. More specifically, it aims to give practice in the skills and language needed in the Reading Comprehension Paper 1 and Composition Paper 2 of the examination. It is ideally suited for use with a full First Certificate course, such as the *Longman First Certificate* course, but is equally useful for the general post-intermediate student who wants to improve his or her reading and writing.

How the book is organised

The book contains 20 Units. The first 18 Units follow the same Unit format, while Units 19 and 20 aim to give final guidance and advice for taking the two Papers.

Units 1–18 are each divided into three parts, A, B and C. Part A aims to help prepare for Reading Comprehension Paper 1; part B 'bridges the gap' between parts A and C; and part C gives careful guidance for Composition Paper 2.

Units 2, 4, 8, 10, 14 and 16 provide specific preparation for Section A of the Reading Comprehension Paper, but **Part A** of all Units gives practice in a variety of reading skills which the exam expects students to have mastered and which are tested through multiple-choice questions in Section B of the Paper.

Part B of each Unit is the 'language link' between parts A and C and gives practice in language (often) presented in reading comprehension passages (part A) and required for composition preparation and writing (part C).

Part C of each Unit is designed to help prepare for Composition Paper 2 and is generally connected with the first part of the Unit by theme or subject. Preparation for the different kinds of First Certificate composition (Letter, Narrative, Description, 'Speech' and Argument) is cycled three or four times (see Contents).

NB: Twenty more composition topics are provided at the end of the book (pages 86–87) for practice in freer composition writing after the more controlled practice given in Units.

How to use the material

Practice in certain exam skills (for example, dealing with multiple-choice questions) is built up slowly over a number of Units, so there are reasons why students are advised to work through the Units in chronological order – though this is not absolutely essential. Indeed, since the preparation for composition writing is carefully cycled, students might instead concentrate on one composition 'type' (letter writing, for example) and work through the Units devoted to that type (in this case Units 1, 6, 11 and 16).

There is no set procedure for Units, but there is one suggestion we would make regarding many of the exercises to be done in class: as often as possible, students should check their answers to exercises with a partner, and then with the rest of the class and the teacher before checking with the Key. This means that students constantly have to justify their answers, choices, opinions etc.

Outside the classroom, **read as much and as widely in English as you can**. The more you read in English, the easier Paper 1 will be.

Special note to the self-access student

1 Following the steps as if you were working in a class, you can do all the Units, except some of the classroom discussion phases.
2 If you do not understand something, look it up in a dictionary or a lexicon.
3 Check your answers in the Key after each exercise. (Unfortunately, because of space, we have not been able to give a model for each composition.)
4 Whenever you can, try to sit down with another student to discuss and compare what you are doing.
5 If you think something is too hard, don't give up. Keep trying.
6 Finally, don't move on to a new Unit until you have got the most from the Unit you are working on. If you do leave a Unit before you have really finished it, come back to it later when you are fresh, and try again!

Contents

Composition Focus Pages *Composition Focus Pages*

UNIT 1   LETTER   6–9
What about coming to see us?

Reading and matching;
True/False exercise;
Language of invitations, thanks
(+ acceptance/refusal + reasons);
Personal letter of invitation

UNIT 2   NARRATIVE   10–13
What happened?

Preparation for Paper 1 Section A;
Inference questions;
Past narrative using *so, because, after, before* and *when*;
Open-ended story (fact or fiction)

UNIT 3   DESCRIPTION   14–17
What's it like?

Identifying source of text;
True/False exercise (with reasons);
has/have been done, had been done and *have something done*;
Describing a house, apartment, etc.

UNIT 4   'SPEECH'   18–21
What's happening?

Preparation for Paper 1 Section A;
True/False exercise (with reasons);
Multiple-choice (with 2 options);
'Position' phrases e.g. *on my left*, and 'ordering' phrases e.g. *First . . ., And then . . .*, for 'speech'

UNIT 5   ARGUMENT   22–25
Are you for or against?

Multiple-choice (with 2 options);
Language to introduce points (e.g. *The first point I would like to make . . .*), add to points (e.g. *What is more, . . .*) and introduce examples;
Argument *for* or *against*

UNIT 6   LETTER   26–29
What's your excuse?

Open-ended questions, including inference;
Multiple-choice (with 3 options);
Language of apologies, excuses, and advice;
Personal letter giving advice

UNIT 7   NARRATIVE   30–33
How did it end?

Open-ended factual questions;
Scanning for numbers and names;
Deducing vocabulary from context;
Story from a 'starter' or 'last sentence'

UNIT 8   DESCRIPTION   34–37
Can you describe the place?

Preparation for Paper 1 Section A;
Identifying source of text;
True/False exercise (with reasons);
Article *the* or no *the*;
Describing your village, town, city

UNIT 9   'SPEECH'   38–41
What can I say?

Multiple-choice (with 4 options);
Deducing vocabulary from context;
Language to exaggerate or emphasise;
before/after doing, while doing, since doing;
Speech of farewell, etc.

UNIT 10   ARGUMENT   42–45
What are the pros and cons?

Preparation for Paper 1 Section A;
Identifying source of text;
Language to contrast ideas e.g. *On the one hand, . . . but on the other . . .*;
Argument *for* and *against*

Composition Focus Pages

UNIT 11   LETTER   46–49

Could you tell me about it?

True/False statements;
Multiple-choice (with 4 options);
Formal and informal letter style;
What I would like to know is . . ., etc.;
Formal letter requesting information

UNIT 12   NARRATIVE   50–53

What did you do next?

Multiple-choice (with 4 options);
Sentence patterns for narrative writing: tenses *did, was/were doing, had done*;
Reporting speech;
Open-ended story (fact or fiction)

UNIT 13   DESCRIPTION   54–57

What do they look like?

True/False with reasons;
Vocabulary to describe people;
Combining facts with *and, as well as, although, despite*, etc.;
Describing a person

UNIT 14   'SPEECH'   58–61

How can I help you?

Preparation for Paper 1 Section A;
Multiple-choice questions;
Language of instructions, advice and warning;
Explaining something to someone

UNIT 15   ARGUMENT   62–65

What's the solution?

Predicting from headline, etc.;
Multiple-choice questions;
Language for posing a question, suggesting a solution and giving examples;
Argument: suggesting a solution

Composition Focus Pages

UNIT 16   LETTER   66–69

What can you do about it?

Preparation for Paper 1 Section A;
Multiple-choice questions;
Language to express annoyance, explain a fault and request action;
Letter of complaint

UNIT 17   NARRATIVE   70–73

What did you use to do?

Multiple-choice questions;
Deducing vocabulary from context;
remember/forget doing;
used to do, would do, etc. for habits;
Narrating past experiences

UNIT 18   ARGUMENT   74–77

What's your own opinion?

Multiple-choice questions;
Language of opinion: *In my view, Some would argue . . ., but as I see it . . .*, etc.;
Argument for *and* against, with opinion

UNIT 19   78–81

How to tackle Paper 1 Reading Comprehension

General instructions
Sample Test Sections A and B
Exam Advice: Golden Rules

UNIT 20   82–85

How to tackle Paper 2 Composition

Exam Guidance for the whole Paper
Exam Advice: Golden Rules
A brief revision of composition writing

Twenty more composition topics   86–87

Key to Exercises

UNIT 1

What about coming to see us?

A1 Below are brief extracts from eight personal letters. Read them quickly to answer this question: What are they all about?

A2 Now, in pairs, read the extracts again and match them. The extracts on the right (a, b, c and d) are answers to those on the left (1, 2, 3 and 4) – but which is the answer to which? or who answered whose letter? How do you know?

1 I shall be delighted to come to your party, but you forgot to say what time it (Jack)

2 I know we haven't seen each other for years and years, but I thought that as I'm coming down (Alan)

3 We were wondering if you'd like to come up and stay with us for (Peter)

4 I'm afraid we won't be able to come on Saturday because (Carole)

a It was so nice to hear from you after all this time. Yes, why don't you (Anna)

b Thank you very much indeed for inviting me to spend the weekend after next with you (Marie)

c How silly of me not to mention the time! We've asked people to arrive any time after eight, but if you can't come until later (Madeleine)

d I'm sorry to hear that you won't be with us this weekend. Perhaps you'd like to (Mohammed)

A3 How do you think each extract continued? In pairs complete the unfinished sentences, then compare your versions with those of other students, like this:

Jack says he'll be delighted to come to your party, but you forgot to say . . .

A4 The extract below is from a personal letter. John is writing to Tony and Jane. Read it and do the exercise on page 7.

Sorry I haven't written for so long, but Mary and I have both been busy looking for new jobs. I probably told you that the hospital where she worked was cutting down on staff, and I have just about had enough of the 'York Daily News'.

The good news is that from the middle of next month I'll be working for a super new company that's just moved up from London. In fact it's a Japanese firm that produces video games, and they'll be giving me a month's training as well as a much bigger salary. (The children are looking forward to Dad bringing home the latest games for their home computer!) This also means, by the way, that Mary won't have to find another job for a month or so: she's felt for some time that she hasn't been spending enough time with the kids – although of course we can't live on my money alone.

The bad news is that we won't be able to come down and see you as planned at the end of this month. Still, as you and Jane do quite a lot of travelling, perhaps it won't be too long before we see you in this part of the world.

Are the following statements true or false? Give reasons.

	T	F
1 John is tired of working for a newspaper.		
2 Mary has probably been asked to leave her job at the hospital.		
3 John will earn a lot more in his new job.		
4 The children are excited about their father's new job.		
5 John and Mary have just moved to London.		
6 Mary will have to find another job immediately.		
7 John and Mary had arranged to visit Tony and Jane.		
8 John invites Tony and Jane to stay with them.		

B1 Here is some of the language we use in order to

a invite someone to something (e.g. an event) or to do something;
b thank someone; and then
c accept or refuse, and give a reason for a refusal.

Study it carefully, cover it and then do exercise **B2**.

Invitation	Would you like/care to [come to a party next Friday]? I/We wonder if you'd like/care to [come to a party next Friday.] (We can also use, for example: We wondered . . ./We were wondering . . .)
Thanks	Thanks (very much) Thank you (very much) (indeed) } for { the invitation [to your party]. I'd/We'd like to thank you inviting me/us [to spend a few days with you].
Acceptance	I'd/We'd love to [come]. I'd/We'd be delighted/very pleased to [come].
Refusal	I'm/We're (very) sorry } (that) we won't/shan't be able to [come]. I'm/We're afraid
Reason	(You see,) the thing is, } unfortunately [we shall be on holiday at that time]. The reason is,

B2 Read the following conversation and fill in the parts which have been left blank. Read the whole conversation first so that you get the gist of what it's about. All the blanks can be filled with expressions from those in **B1**.

John: Hello, Mike. Hello, Ann. I'm glad I've met you. I was going to ring you later. Susan and I were wondering _____ (1)?
Mike: The theatre? That sounds a nice idea. Thanks _____ (2) I'd _____ (3).
John: What about you, Ann? We've got tickets for Saturday night. Would _____ (4)?
Ann: Well, thanks _____ (5), but I'm afraid _____ (6).
John: Oh, that's a shame. Why not?
Ann: Unfortunately I'm going to London for the weekend. Perhaps another time.

UNIT 1

C1 Read this letter. Then complete what John said to his wife Mary after he had read it quickly. Begin: 'I've just had a letter from Tony and Jane. They . . .'

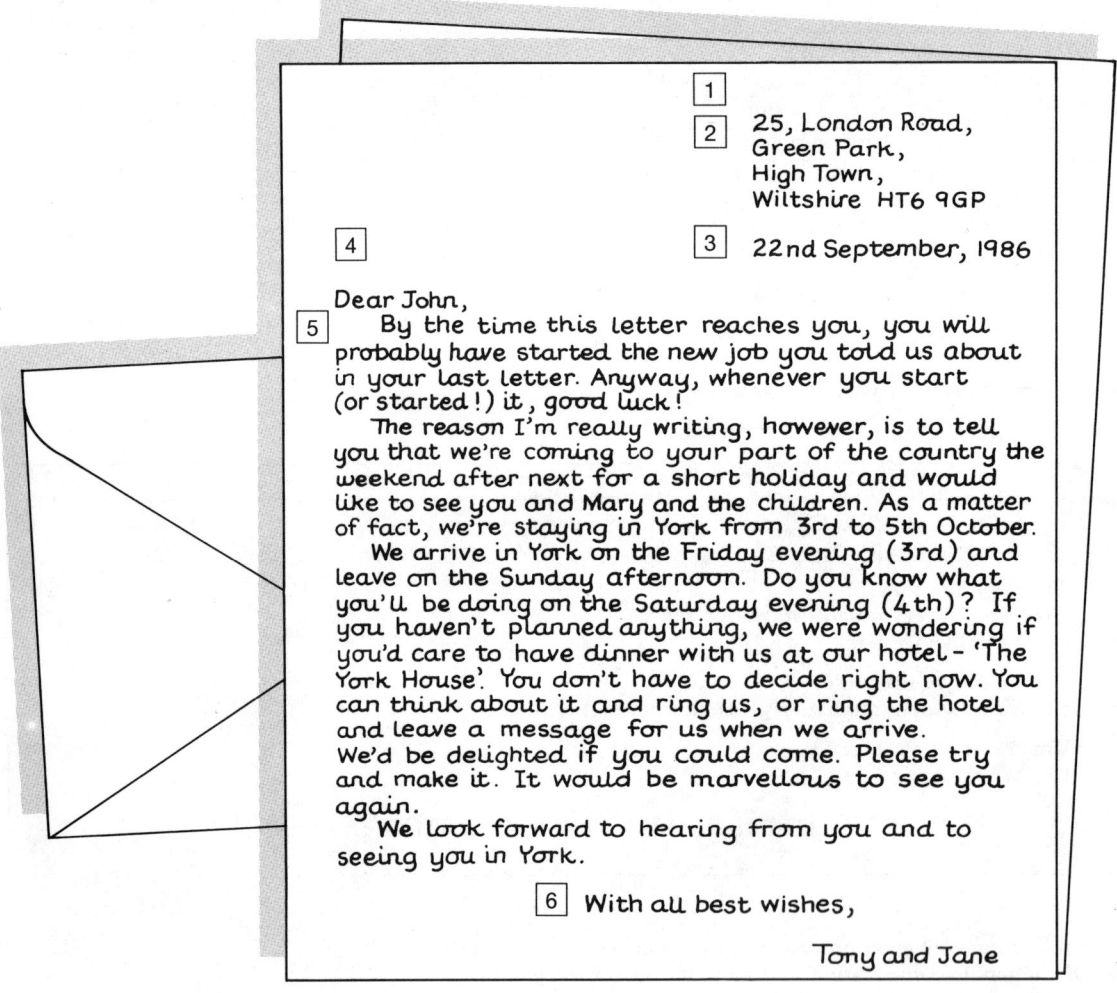

```
                                    ┌─┐
                                    │1│
                                    ├─┤ 25, London Road,
                                    │2│ Green Park,
                                        High Town,
                                        Wiltshire HT6 9GP
              ┌─┐                   ┌─┐
              │4│                   │3│ 22nd September, 1986
              └─┘                   └─┘
        Dear John,
  ┌─┐     By the time this letter reaches you, you will
  │5│   probably have started the new job you told us about
        in your last letter. Anyway, whenever you start
        (or started!) it, good luck!
          The reason I'm really writing, however, is to tell
        you that we're coming to your part of the country the
        weekend after next for a short holiday and would
        like to see you and Mary and the children. As a matter
        of fact, we're staying in York from 3rd to 5th October.
          We arrive in York on the Friday evening (3rd) and
        leave on the Sunday afternoon. Do you know what
        you'll be doing on the Saturday evening (4th)? If
        you haven't planned anything, we were wondering if
        you'd care to have dinner with us at our hotel - 'The
        York House'. You don't have to decide right now. You
        can think about it and ring us, or ring the hotel
        and leave a message for us when we arrive.
        We'd be delighted if you could come. Please try
        and make it. It would be marvellous to see you
        again.
          We look forward to hearing from you and to
        seeing you in York.

                    ┌─┐
                    │6│  With all best wishes,

                                         Tony and Jane
```

C2 The letter above is a personal letter. It is fairly informal, but the layout is still important. What do you notice about it? Cover the comments on the right and discuss the questions on the left. Then check with the comments.

Questions

1 What don't you write at the top of an English letter?

2 What do you notice about the address in English?

Comments

1 You never write your name at the top of a personal English letter.* Your signature at the bottom tells the reader who the letter is from.

2 The address is written in the top right-hand corner: name of house (if it has one), then house number and street/road, town/city, county, post code, and country (if writing to someone abroad). Note the use of capital letters with places and months.

8

3 What do you notice about the date in English? Where does it normally appear? How else can you write it?

3 The date appears under your address and there are different forms you can use, for example: 1st April, 1988; 1 April 1988; April 1st, 1988; 1–4–'88; 1/4/88. Note the use of commas in the address and the date.

4 Do *all* English letters begin with 'Dear + First name'?

4 No. Most begin with 'Dear . . .', but you only use a person's first name in a personal letter. Other letters begin 'Dear Mr/Mrs/Miss/Ms/Dr etc. + family name' or 'Dear Sir/Madam/Sirs/Sir or Madam, etc.' Note the comma after 'Dear John,'.

5 What do you notice about the 'body' or main part of the letter?

5 It has three main parts: an introduction (paragraph 1), the message (here, paragraphs 2 and 3), and a conclusion.

6 Do *all* English letters end with something like 'With all best wishes, + First name(s)'?

6 No, only friendly letters, which may end with phrases such as 'Best wishes', 'See you', '(Lots of) love' + first name. Other letters end with 'Yours faithfully' or 'Yours sincerely'.

> * There is one time when you might put a name at the top of a personal letter, and that is if you are, for example, staying with an English family as a student and add the letters 'c/o' (= care of, or staying at), like this:
>
> c/o Mrs J. Smith,
> 35, High Street,
> Small Town BX3 TH13
> England

C3 Write out the following addresses and dates (with months in writing), with the correct punctuation and layout, as if for the top of a personal letter:

1 the firs / 54 larkshill road / little village / northington / surrey / 21–3–87
2 flat 6 / 178 bristol road / southtown / yorkshire YY3 5AB / 19–10–'86
3 163 westwood avenue / east moors / ringwood / hampshire 12T B34 / 3–7–87
4 c o mr and mrs james / 57 long drive / exbourne / kent / england / 23–5–'87

C4 Here is a typical First Certificate letter-writing task. Write the letter, paying careful attention to the layout, and using some of the prompts to guide you. First ask yourself two questions: what address are you going to use – your home address or a fictional one? – and who are you writing to?

Paragraph 1
Thank friend for letter and tickets. Kind of him/her to think of you. Obviously remembered how much you like classical music.

Paragraph 2
Regret you won't be able to go. Say why – for example, another appointment that evening, or away on holiday/business? Add: *I'm returning the tickets in plenty of time, as I think* . . . Who do you think would like the chance to go?

Paragraph 3
Thank the friend once again. Add: *See you soon, All best wishes,* and sign it with your first name.

> 'A friend has just sent you a short letter enclosing two free tickets to a classical concert in ten days' time. Write a letter expressing your thanks, but giving reasons why you will not be able to go. Return the tickets and suggest someone else who might enjoy the concert.'

C5 Why not try composition 1 on page 86 as well?

UNIT 2

What happened?

A1 Section A of the First Certificate Reading Comprehension Paper 1 contains 25 multiple-choice items like the ones below. The correct answer may depend on the grammar of the sentence, on the kind of word needed (an adjective, adverb, noun, etc.), on collocation (the way a word is always used with another word), etc. Study number 1 and the answer and reason below, then do items 2–5 and discuss your answers, giving reasons.

> 1 I knew they had _____ me too much in the shop when I noticed that the price tag said 75p and I had paid 85p.
> **A** afforded **B** charged **C** cost **D** spent

Choice **B** is the correct answer. Why?

Although all four verbs are to do with money, only the verb *charge* fits here, meaning *ask someone for a stated amount of money for something*.

2 He took his _____ to the watchmaker's to have the metal strap adjusted.
 A clock **B** alarm **C** wristwatch **D** clockwork

3 I _____ meeting at 7.00, but the others thought that 7.30 would be better.
 A arranged **B** suggested **C** appointed **D** put forward

4 After she moved house she couldn't find her umbrella anywhere, but she felt absolutely sure it would _____ eventually.
 A emerge **B** come out **C** arrive **D** turn up

5 John's _____ employer refused to give him a reference for his new job.
 A before **B** soon **C** previous **D** lastly

A2 The following text is from a newspaper. Read it as quickly as you can and answer these questions:

1 What's it about?   2 Can you give it a headline?

> How about this for service? I took a wristwatch into a jeweller's here in town to be repaired. On Monday I collected it. Nothing unusual in that, you might say, until I tell you when I took it in to be mended.
>   It was twenty-six years ago! I was not then 15 years old and I forgot to collect it. Months went by and I hadn't the nerve to go in and ask for it. I left it so long I thought they must have sold it. But on Monday I had cause to go into the shop again, so I asked, on the off-chance, whether it was still there.
>   Sure enough, the son of the previous owner of the shop found it for me. It still had on it the ticket in my maiden name which was put on it, by his father! The jeweller said his record for holding a watch before was eight years, so he suggested I write to you about it.
>   I wasn't charged a penny. I think the jeweller was so surprised that I had turned up after all those years.
>
> *Daily Mirror*

A3 Now read the text again and answer these questions. The answers are clearly given somewhere in the text.

1 What did the writer take into the jeweller's? Why?
2 When had the writer taken it in?
3 How old was the writer at the time?
4 What was the longest time the jeweller had held a watch before that?
5 How much did the writer have to pay to have the watch repaired?

A4 Read the text once more to find answers to these questions. The information you need here is not so clear: *you have to infer or deduce the answers.*

1 Was the writer a man or a woman? How do you know?
2 Had the jeweller bought the shop from a stranger? Again, how do you know?
3 How old is the writer now?

A5 Look at this part of the text from page 10 in which words have been left out.
Read it with the words that have been filled in and the kinds of questions you should ask about the blanks – what kind of word is missing? what went before? what comes after? and so on.
Then fill in the other blanks in the same way, and check with the original text.

How about this for service? I took a wristwatch ___into___ (1) a jeweller's here in town to ___be___ (2) repaired. ___On___ (3) Monday I collected it. Nothing unusual in that, you ___might___ (4) say, until I tell you when I took _____ (5) in to be mended.
It was twenty-six years _____ (6)! I was not then 15 years _____ (7) and I forgot to collect it. Months went _____ (8) and I hadn't the nerve to go in and ask _____ (9) it. I left it so long I thought they must _____ (10) sold it. But on Monday I had cause to go into the shop again, _____ (11) I asked, on the off-chance, _____ (12) it was still there.

1 What kind of word is missing? A preposition – a word like *for, to, at, on, by*, etc. It follows the verb *took*, so it must be a 'direction' preposition – *to* or *into*.
2 What kind of word is missing? It must be a verb, after *to* (= in order to) – *be* or *have*. It can't be *have*: it would have to read 'to _____ it repaired'. So it must be *be*.
3 When did the writer collect the watch? _____ Monday. Prepositions of time: *in* (+ year or month), *at* (+ time), *on* (+ day). So it's *on*. Or possibly: *Last*.
4 What kind of word can go between *you* and *say*? A word like *will, can, must, would*, etc. And what would make sense here? – a choice: *may, might, could*, – even *will*.

A6 For fun, work in pairs and take it in turns to read out more sentences from the same text, leaving blanks (and using the word 'blank'), like this:

'Sure enough, the son of the previous BLANK of the shop found BLANK for me.'

B One of the composition types in the First Certificate is a story. It might be fact or fiction – something that really happened to you in the past, or a story you make up or imagine. But before you prepare to write one, here are two exercises to help you with some of the kinds of sentences you might use. Notice the tenses that are used.

B1 **so** or **because**?

Join the following pairs of sentences – once with *so* and once with *because*.

Example: I had had a hard day. When I got home, I went straight to bed.

You write: *I had had a hard day* **so**, *when I got home, I went straight to bed.*
and: *I went straight to bed when I got home* **because** *I had had a hard day.*

1 I had plenty of time. I didn't hurry.
2 She was very worried. She asked her friend for some advice.
3 The man went to prison. The man was found guilty of stealing.
4 I was lost. I asked a passer-by the way to the Town Hall.
5 I thought I was going to be late for my appointment. I called a taxi.

B2 **after, before** and **when**

Join these pairs of sentences – once with *before* and once with *after* or *when*.

Example: He put out the lights. Then he locked the door.

You write: *He put out the lights* **before** *he locked the door.*
and: *He locked the door* **after/when** *he had put out the lights.*

1 I checked the contents. Then I locked my suitcase.
2 The journalist heard the judge's verdict. Then he rang his newspaper.
3 They watched the film. Then they began their discussion.
4 She went to see the doctor. Then she phoned her office.
5 I read all about the computer. Then I went and bought one.

C1 Here is a typical First Certificate composition of this kind:

> 'Write what happened when you were delayed on the way to an important meeting, and what you did to inform those concerned that you would be late.'

Your first decision: Are you going to write about a *real* event?
or are you going to make up a story?

When you've decided, answer the following questions to guide you in writing your story. The words and phrases on the right are there to help you to put your ideas together and *to make what you write sound English.*

Paragraph 1
When did this happen (to you)?
(Remember: *in 1973, in July 1980, in early spring 1976, during the winter of 1976, last year, (about) ten years ago*, etc.)

Why will you always remember it?
or Why will you never forget it?
Where were you going?/ What were you supposed to be attending?
Where was the meeting?

Who was the meeting with?

Paragraph 2
When was the meeting arranged for?

Did you think you had plenty of time? Why?
Did you hurry or not?
What time did you leave your house or apartment?
What did you do – go to catch the bus? walk to the station? get out your bicycle/motorbike/car?

Paragraph 3
Was that when the trouble started? or later? [For this exercise, let's assume it started then.]
What happened? How long had you been waiting for the bus/walking/riding/driving when it happened?
What did you think? Did you think you still had plenty of time, or did you think the delay would make you late?
What did you decide to do? Did you look for some other form of transport? Did you look around for a telephone? Why?
Did you find, or couldn't you find, any other transport, or a telephone?

Paragraph 4
Did you manage to get a message through to them finally?
Did you send your apologies? Did you explain briefly why you had been held up? And did you promise anything? – e.g. to get there as soon as you could?

What I'm going to tell you about happened (to me) . . . [when?]
or This happened to me . . . [when?]
or The experience I'm going to write about happened [when?]
I shall always remember it/I shall never forget it because . . . [why?]
I was going to a/an . . . /I was supposed to be attending a/an . . . [what?]
. . . in/at/near/not far from/about (10) kilometres from . . . [where?]
with . . . [whom?]

. . . [what time of day? e.g. 10 o'clock in the morning? 3 in the afternoon?]
Naturally I thought . . . because . . .
. . . so . . .
I left . . . [time?]
. . . and . . . [what?]

That was . . .

I had been . . . [doing what?] . . . for . . . [how long?] . . . when . . . [what happened?]
I immediately thought . . . [what?]

. . . so . . . [what?]

. . . so that . . . [why?]

Eventually I managed . . .

I sent . . . [what?] and explained . . .

C2 Why not try composition 2 on page 86?

An important note
The instructions for the First Certificate Composition Paper say that the two compositions you write 'must be between 120 and 180 words each'. That's not very long – in fact the short article in **A2** (page 10) is just over 180 words – so you can take time to plan what you want to write and take care when writing. It also means that you have time to check your work carefully when you have finished.

UNIT 3

What's it like?

A1 In Section B of the Reading Comprehension Paper 1 you may have to answer questions about three texts on the same subject but from different sources.
These descriptions are taken from different sources – a personal letter, a novel, etc. Read them carefully and say where each comes from and why.

1 The stage is divided into two areas. Stage left is Harry's bedroom with single bed upstage left. There are clothes littering the floor, and the walls are covered with Impressionist prints. Stage right: kitchen and living area, sofa, old armchair and a bookcase full of large hardback volumes along back wall.

2 Follow in the footsteps of Kings and Queens. Wander at your leisure around the delightful grounds on the banks of the gently-flowing Stour. Climb the historic Forest Tower and feast your eyes on the picturesque surrounding countryside. Marvel at the superb State Rooms including the magnificent 15th-century Hall.

3 The cottage is a dream. Can't believe our luck! The children can't get over the oak-panelled staircase and attic. Perfect for their hide and seek! There are low ceilings and solid beams everywhere, and it's got a super stone-floor kitchen, a cosy lounge, and French windows leading out onto a really delightful garden. It's like something out of a fairy tale.

4 Fire broke out in a five-bedroomed detached house in Derby Avenue in the early hours of Tuesday morning. Firemen were called to deal with a blaze, thought to have been started by a gas explosion, that had neighbours worried for their own safety. The owners of the splendid 18th-century house are believed to be on a touring holiday in France, and attempts were being made today to contact them.
According to eye-witnesses, flames swept through the building in minutes and the first-floor rooms, some apparently containing valuable antique furniture, were completely gutted. It is estimated that at least £45,000 worth of damage was done.

5 I was born in the master bedroom (I am reliably informed) of a semi-detached house on the outskirts of Bridlington. We moved to the south coast before I started school, but I still have some recollection of this first home.
Apart from the room in which I was brought into the world, the house had two other smaller bedrooms which slept all four of us children. There was a dark, dingy kitchen and a much brighter sitting room where every Sunday afternoon visitors would be received. There was a small overgrown vegetable garden at the back, complete with outside toilet and a tumbledown shed, where my father used to escape from my mother's religion (or so he told me later), and a much tidier front garden facing on to the street. My parents, especially my mother, always believed in keeping up appearances.

A2 Which of the people below do you think live, lived or might live in four of the houses described? Say why you think so.

a Dr and Mrs Smythe-Welby and their three teenage children.
b Harry and Sue Matthews and their school-age children while on holiday.
c Lord and Lady Beaumont and their five-man staff.
d H.D. Campbell, a university student.

A3 Look carefully at extract 4 again. Which words, phrases or lines indicate that

1 this is not from a national paper?
2 it is from an evening newspaper?
3 no one was hurt in the fire?
4 the house owners were well-off?
5 no criminal action was involved?
6 it was not a new house?
7 it was not a bungalow?
8 some people were awake when the fire started?

A4 Look carefully at extract 5 again. Are the following statements true or false? Give reasons.

1 Bridlington is probably situated on the south coast.
2 The writer spent most of his childhood in that house.
3 He had four brothers and sisters.
4 His father was less religious than his mother.
5 His mother did not want the front garden to look untidy.
6 There was very little space in the house.

B1 Describing a house or a room requires an 'eye for detail' and some fairly precise descriptive vocabulary. Check you know the words in the box (look them up in a dictionary if necessary), then put them in the gaps in this extract.

cracked	faded	damp
stained	rusty	peeled
worn	torn	twisted
dust	grease	

   I stood for a moment at the top of the stairs, looking up at a few (1) _____ wires which presumably had once helped to provide a decent light for the landing. She pushed open the door for me and I looked inside. The carpet was very (2) _____, the curtains were (3) _____ in places and were (4) _____ with what looked like blood or red ink. All the paintwork had (5) _____ to a brownish yellow and there were large (6) _____ patches on three of the walls, with the result that most of the wallpaper had (7) _____ off. I moved across the room. Every pane of glass was (8) _____ and the metal catches were so (9) _____ I was sure the window had not been opened for years. There was a thick layer of (10) _____ on the furniture and an equally thick layer of (11) _____ on the cooker in the tiny kitchen area.
   'How much did you say it was?' I asked.
   '£35 a week,' the woman replied.
   'I'll take it,' I said, much to her surprise.

UNIT 3

B2 Apart from interesting vocabulary, a descriptive composition should have more varied structures than simply *It is . . ., It has . . ., There is . . .,* and *There are . . .*, although of course you can use them. Look carefully at these examples:

> My sister has completely transformed her kitchen. Solid wood cupboards have been fitted all along one wall and the other walls have been tiled from top to bottom.
>
> When I drove past my old house last year, I hardly recognised it. The stonework had been painted bright pink and a new roof had been put on.

Now build on the following situations in the same way. Make sure you choose correctly between *has/have been done* and *had been done* in each case.

1 By the end of the year their garden looked much better.
 (all the rubbish / clear away; nice evergreen bushes / plant)
2 There's a much cosier atmosphere in our lounge now.
 (the centre light / replace by wall lights; old fashioned fireplace / put in)
3 I was amazed when they invited me back to look round the office in 1981.
 (all the furniture / move around; new photocopier, computer, coffee machine install)
4 Make sure you don't get lost if you go upstairs to their toilet.
 (two rooms / convert into one; small bedroom / turn into shower room)

These 'stories' could also be told using the structure *have something done*:

> My sister has completely transformed her kitchen. *She's had solid wood cupboards fitted* all along one wall and *she's had the other walls tiled* from top to bottom.
>
> When I drove past my old house last year, I hardly recognised it. *The new owners had had the stonework painted* bright pink and *(they'd had) a new roof put on.*

Go through situations 1–4 again and express the ideas using this structure.

B3 Imagine you have been shown round a house that you're interested in renting and you're talking about your impressions now. There are some problems. For example:

'The grass is very long. It needs cutting.'

Make similar comments with these prompts:

1 windows – clean
2 wooden floors – polish
3 curtains – wash
4 door hinges – oil
5 woodwork – paint
6 some floorboards – nail down
7 carpets – shampoo
8 some furniture – repair

C1 Look at the picture of the castle below and write a piece for a publicity brochure to go with it. Refer back to the language used in extract 2 on page 14, and consider the verbs in the box to start your sentences.

If you want to, think of a castle or a palace that you know in your country, and write about that.

Begin like this:

'Enjoy a day out in a 14th-century castle!'

enjoy	picnic	look around
relax	admire	visit
stroll	see	have lunch
climb	wander	marvel at

C2 Write the middle part of a personal letter in which you tell an English-speaking friend about the new house or apartment that you (and your family?) have just moved into. The following notes and questions should help you.

Paragraph 1
Say something about when, why and how you moved house.
How did you feel about leaving your old home?
And how do you feel about starting life in a new one?

Paragraph 2
Describe the house or apartment and the different rooms. (e.g. 'The house is situated . . .'; 'The lounge is furnished . . .'; 'The kitchen is now equipped with . . .')
What furniture have you (or your family) put in different rooms?
How have you decorated it? Or how have you had it decorated?

Paragraph 3
Mention some of the things that are not in good order – some of the things that need doing.
What are you going to do or have done (or what have you already done, or had done) to make the place more comfortable or to give it more 'character'?

Paragraph 4
Invite your friend to come and visit you, perhaps when you have sorted everything out and have really settled in.

UNIT 4

What's happening?

A1 In Section A of the Reading Comprehension Paper 1, there can be a number of reasons why one answer is right and the other three choices wrong. Sometimes, as in the items below, the clue is in another word or phrase in the sentence.
Study this example, then do items 2–5.

> 1 Fortunately the car was only _____ damaged in the crash.
>   **A** seriously **B** slightly **C** badly **D** terribly

Choice **B** is the correct answer. Why?

The words *fortunately* and *only* tell us that the accident was not too bad. **A**, **C** and **D**, although they can go with *damaged*, would suggest a bad crash. *Slightly* means *a little*, so it's the perfect word here.

2 I was _____ to find that my favourite vase had been smashed to pieces.
  A delighted **B** horrified **C** frustrated **D** proud

3 I tried to change that stubborn man's mind, but it was a _____ task.
  A hopeless **B** simple **C** sceptical **D** victorious

4 Surprisingly the explosion was quite _____.
  A loud **B** quiet **C** strange **D** deafening

5 Nothing much happens here _____ the occasional party.
  A not to mention **B** apart from **C** as well as **D** including

A2 Now quickly read the extract below and answer this one question:

Where is the writer sitting?

Don't worry at this stage about any vocabulary you do not understand.

We are waiting for the next attack. Presumably the last. The high-pitched screams and deafening explosions of the recent battle are still ringing in my ears. Apart from that, there is a strange silence all around me: total silence except for the whirring of the monitors recording our position and the occasional update from Mission Control. These are not acknowledged as our intercom lies smashed to pieces on the floor.

There is no sign of the Multicon fleet on our screens, but we know they cannot be far away. They must know they outnumber us. And yet they have not come to finish us off. Did we inflict more damage than we thought? Wishful thinking, no doubt.

To my left Crewmember McKilroy is twiddling the bank of dials in front of him in a hopeless attempt to repair our damaged medium-range missiles. He looks strangely like a young boy frustrated by a home video game that is beyond him. His right eye is developing a twitch, I see. Despite all his training, then, he is beginning to feel the pressure.

I can hear Mission Control assuring the world's media that we are safe and well, and not far short of victory. 'They have suffered some losses, but our flagship is preparing to take on the enemy and . . ..' Some losses!

I can see a meteorite gliding past on my right; in other circumstances we would have been horrified by its closeness. Far below us the rings of Saturn are clearly visible. And far far away I can see a little boy sitting on a garden swing and can hear him saying to his sceptical mother: 'I want to be an astronaut when I grow up and save the world and . . ..'

Two Multicon craft are appearing on our screens. I can hear something clicking, faster and faster . . .

A3 Now read it again more carefully and decide whether these statements are true or false. Give reasons.

1. The last battle ended a long time ago.
2. All of their equipment is broken.
3. They can hear Mission Control but can't be heard by them.
4. They have fewer 'ships' than the Multicons.
5. The writer doesn't really believe they did a lot of damage to the enemy.
6. Crewmember McKilroy probably won't be able to repair the missiles.
7. McKilroy is showing signs of nervousness.
8. Mission Control is telling reporters the truth.
9. The writer is shocked to see the meteorite so close.
10. The Multicon craft bring the writer back to the present.

A4 See if you can deduce the meanings of some new words from their context. Which of the words or phrases underlined are connected with sound or noises? How do you know?

A5 In Section B of the Reading Comprehension Paper, you have to answer multiple-choice questions about texts. Sometimes the choices are answers to a question. (In the exam there are always four choices, but to start you off, we're giving only two.)
Look at this example, and then do and discuss items 2–5.

THE QUESTION

1 Why don't they answer Mission Control?

THE CHOICES OR OPTIONS

A Because they can't hear them properly.
B Because their intercom is broken.

A is wrong because they *can* hear 'the occasional update from Mission Control'.
B is correct. The text says their 'intercom lies smashed to pieces on the floor'.

2 What are they waiting for?
   A The enemy fleet to return.
   B Help to arrive from Earth.

3 Why is McKilroy's attempt hopeless?
   A The missiles can't be repaired.
   B He doesn't understand the dials.

4 Who are Mission Control talking to?
   A Reporters.
   B The enemy.

5 Why aren't they worried by the meteorite?
   A It isn't going to pass close to them.
   B They have enough to worry about.

B1 In the examination, you may be asked to write a commentary on what is happening in a particular situation. To do this you will need a number of 'position' phrases like these:

	far above me	high up in the sky
to/on my left		
	in the distance	
	on the horizon	to/on my right
not far from here		
	directly in front of me	
	straight ahead of me	
beyond the trees		just round the corner
on the other side of the road		
		near (to) me
right here	opposite me	behind that house
nearby		way over there
close by		
	all around me	
	a long way below me	

This is how some of them might be used in a radio commentary:

> The noise all around me now is deafening. Just in front of me there's a group singing the National Anthem at the tops of their voices and further along to my right I can see children who can't be more than four or five sitting happily on their fathers' shoulders and joining in.
> To my right and left there's a sea of red, white and blue as flags, scarves and banners are waved in the air. On the far side of the street hundreds of people are leaning out of office windows, and below me the police are having a hard job keeping the crowds behind the barriers.
> Far above me the television helicopters are hovering over the procession route, and in the distance I think I can see them coming. Yes, here they are: on the other side of Parliament Square, we can see the royal coach approaching . . .

Following that style, how would you describe the scene and what is happening in these situations? Use these prompts with the 'position' phrases opposite.

1 You are half-way up a mountain with a climbing expedition, as an observer:
(the peaks – covered in cloud / the leading climbers – approaching the summit / other climbers – cooking, putting up tent, tidying equipment / in tiny village – people like ants)

2 You are a reporter at the scene of a street riot:
(rioters – chanting, shouting, throwing stones / police – linking arms, carrying shields, on horseback trying to disperse the crowd / bystanders – rushing, pushing, screaming, trying to escape)

B2 Another thing you might have to write in the examination is your talk to a group of people telling them the arrangements for a day trip or an afternoon visit, etc.
For this task, 'ordering' phrases like these will be useful:

First, . . .; (And) then, . . .; (And) when we've [done that], . . .;
Afterwards, . . .;
Next, . . .; A little later, . . .; (But) before we [do that], . . .; (And) finally, ...

See how they are used in this short talk:

Write similar short pieces for the following situations. Use these prompts, the ordering phrases above, and add your own ideas.

1 You are the organiser of a student visit to spend a day with a city orchestra:
(meet members of orchestra / attend rehearsal / travel to concert hall / go backstage / meet conductor / watch concert)

2 You are a courier in a city with a group of tourists:
(visit art galleries / museums / go on sightseeing tour by coach / lunch / free for shopping / meet for dinner / evening cruise on river / disco)

> Good morning, ladies and gentlemen. Welcome to the offices of *The Daily News*.
> Now first, we're going to meet the Personnel Manager and she'll take us on a tour of the offices. Then we'll spend some time with the journalists, who'll be putting the final touches to their articles. When we've had morning coffee with them, we'll have a chance to see the editorial staff making any last-minute changes that are necessary, and after that, before we leave, we'll be taken down to the printing presses, and if we're lucky we'll see the first edition actually being printed. Finally, there'll be a photo session and who knows, you may find a picture of yourselves staring out at you from tomorrow's front page.

C1 Now plan and write this composition. Write between 120 and 180 words.

> 'You are showing some English-speaking friends around a local festival which is held in your home town or village every year. Write down what you say as you take them round and point out the events and attractions.'

C2 And why not try composition 4 on page 86 as well?

UNIT 5

Are you for or against?

A1 Read this letter quite quickly, then say what you think the 'recent editorial' was about and what point of view it expressed.

Dear Sir,

I was surprised to read your recent editorial on the question of students' part-time jobs. You appear to be making a lot of generalisations on the basis of just one unfortunate incident. (I assure you that not all young people who deliver newspapers are as foolish and dishonest as the two youths mentioned in your article.)

The first point I would like to make is that there are many jobs teenagers can do which give them useful experience of the working world. They are brought into contact with a variety of people, often older, and are given experience of expressing themselves clearly and coherently. I am thinking here of jobs such as travel guides and shop assistants.

Another argument for schoolchildren and college students having holiday or weekend jobs is that many parents need the financial assistance. If we take, for example, a family in which the father is unemployed or perhaps a single-parent family on a low income, it seems logical and fair that a son or daughter should try to bring money into the household.

One further thing I want to say is that a lot of jobs for the young can be fun for the people who do them and also useful to the community. Youngsters who help in schools, hospitals and with the elderly often derive a great deal of pleasure and satisfaction as well as contributing something valuable to local society.

In conclusion, I would add that when I was a girl, my father said my teens were a time for books, hobbies and academic studies. Thinking back, I feel I would have learnt much more — about myself, other people and life in general — if he had allowed me to do a limited amount of 'real work'. Certainly, when she is old enough, I shall encourage my own daughter to do so, rather than waste her time with soap operas, computer games and discotheques, like so many young people today.

Yours faithfully,

Margaret Williams (Mrs)

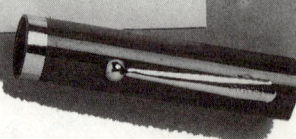

A2 In Unit 4, Section **A5**, you chose answers to a question. Sometimes you must choose the right way to complete a sentence. Look at this example, then do and discuss items 2–6.

THE STEM

> 1 When Mrs Williams says she was surprised, she means

THE CHOICES OR OPTIONS

> A she was pleased to read about the subject.
> B she didn't think the article was right.

A is wrong; she was probably angry rather than pleased about what she read.
B is correct; she thinks the newspaper was generalising unfairly.

2 When she talks about the two youths, she says that
  A they were not to blame.
  B they were not typical.

3 She feels that working as a travel guide will help a young person
  A to see the world.
  B to learn to communicate.

4 In the third paragraph she mentions two families as examples of
  A households with relatively little money.
  B parents losing their jobs to young people.

5 In the fourth paragraph her main point is that young people can
  A have fun while they are working in schools.
  B help themselves and others by working.

6 When she talks about her daughter, Mrs Williams makes it clear that she will
  A bring her up in the same way that she was brought up.
  B encourage her to make good use of her time as a teenager.

A3 Discuss these questions and do the exercises with a partner or in small groups.

1 Mrs Williams' argument has three main points. In which three paragraphs do they appear?
2 Summarise in three short sentences the contents of paragraphs 2, 3 and 4. (Look for the main sentence in each paragraph.)
3 Mrs Williams gives a number of examples to illustrate her points. What are these examples of?
  – travel guides and shop assistants.
  – a family in which the father is unemployed or perhaps a single-parent family on a low income.
  – in schools, hospitals and with the elderly.
  – books, hobbies and academic studies.
  – soap operas, computer games and discotheques.
4 How is the last paragraph different in content from the others?

B One of the composition types you can choose in the First Certificate is a discursive composition, or an 'argument'. For example, you may be asked to argue for *or* against an idea or proposal. Study these three groups of phrases: they will help you to structure an argument. Do the short exercise after each group.

B1 Introducing points in an argument

The first point I would like to make is that . . .

Another { (important) reason / (strong) argument } { for [doing . . ./not doing . . .] / why we should/should not [do . . .] / for [doing . . ./not doing . . .] / against [doing . . .] } is that . . .

One final thing (that) I want to say/which should be said is that . . .

(And) last but not least/And finally { we should remember / we must bear in mind / we must not forget } that . . .

Use some of the expressions above to build an argument for paying everybody the same wages or salary. Here are some points for you to make:
– all people work about the same number of hours.
– all jobs are important.
– unskilled work is not as much fun as skilled work – why pay less?
– most religions say that people should be treated equally.

B2 Developing and adding to points

What is more, . . .
What is even more important is that . . .
What is equally important is the fact that . . .
This applies not only to . . . but also to . . .

Try to develop each of the sentences you made in **B1**, using one of these 'starters'.

B3 Introducing examples

If we take . . ., for example/for instance, it is obvious that . . .
I am thinking here particularly of . . ., such as . . .
There is/There are . . ., not to mention . . .
(And) apart from . . ., there are also . . ., such as/like . . .

Let's say you have just stated in your composition that there are a lot of people who don't earn very much. Give examples, using the phrases above.

C1 Here is a typical First Certificate 'argument' composition:

> 'Give reasons why boarding schools are not the best form of education.'

Use the 'starters', notes and questions to help you write the composition. You must argue *against* boarding schools – whatever you may think personally!

Paragraph 1
The first thing I would like to say is that . . .
I strongly believe that . . .

(Children need parental influence)
(In what ways do children need it?)
(What can happen if they don't have it?)

Paragraph 2
Another strong argument against . . .
What is equally important is (the fact) that . . .
This of course can result in . . .

(Pupils lose touch with the real world)
(They only meet a certain type of person)
(What can be the consequences?)

Paragraph 3
One final point I want to make is that . . .
I am thinking here particularly of . . .

(No contact with members of the opposite sex)
(What type of school?)

Paragraph 4
In conclusion, I would say that . . .

(Day schools have many advantages)
(Will you send your children to a boarding school?)

C2 In this final task, we are not going to suggest which phrases you use. We are giving you some points to choose from. (There may be too many to include in a short composition.) Choose from the language on page 24 to introduce and connect your points. Your composition topic is:

> 'Write a composition of between 120 and 180 words, giving reasons why school and college students should not do part-time work.'

Paragraph 1
– being a student is a full-time job – a great deal to do e.g. homework, background reading, research and project work
– need a lot of energy and concentration
– a job is a distraction – can't study so well – leads to extra pressure

Paragraph 2
– there are dangers e.g. young people can be exploited – work for almost nothing, out late at night or early morning, often have contact with strangers e.g. delivering newspapers, door-to-door selling

Paragraph 3
– a working life of 40 years is long enough – why make it longer?
– increases unemployment by taking jobs adults could do

Paragraph 4
– young people should broaden their interests, develop hobbies, etc.
– not spend hours doing boring work to save to buy new shoes, etc.
– also spend more time with family – keep the family unit strong

UNIT 6

What's your excuse?

A1 This is an extract from a novel. Read it and answer this question:
What kind of novel do you think it comes from? Give reasons.

James Read unlocked the front door absent-mindedly and stepped from the cold foggy night into the warm hallway of his own home. He was still thinking about the meeting. It had not gone at all well, and had not lasted very long, mainly because Ray Wallace had not been present. And what had surprised most of those attending was that James, as Chairman, had not received an apology from him, verbal or written. 'Very strange,' James thought to himself as he switched on the light. 'Not like Ray at all, especially since –'

His thoughts were cut short by the sight of an envelope on the mat just inside the door. He had stepped over it as he entered in the dark. He bent down, picked it up and looked at it. On the front, in hastily scrawled handwriting was his name: that was all. 'Obviously delivered by hand.' He ambled into the lounge, sat down at his desk, turned on the lamp and sat back. He opened the envelope and pulled out a letter. Unfolding it, he read:

> 'The Vicarage',
> Lytch Lane,
> Deverill
>
> 10th May 1963
>
> Dear James,
> Please accept my (now somewhat belated) apologies for not attending the meeting this evening. However, I feel sure that you and the others will forgive me when you read what has occurred. (I will also apologise for my handwriting, but this must be written in some haste – speed is of the essence now!)
> Just before I was about to leave the hotel to come to the meeting, I received another 'communication' from the kidnapper. It just said: 'This is the girl's last chance. Come to the churchyard at 11.30 with £10,000. Come alone. We are watching you.' As usual, he (or she?) signed it with the 'Evil Eye' –
>
>
>
> Clearly I had to make careful preparations, so I came to the vicarage first to have a good look at the churchyard once again. The vicar has kindly lent me the use of his desk and writing things.
> You would be well advised not to contact the others on the committee. My instinct tells me there is one we should not trust.
> But you can put your trust in me. *We shall get Alana back unharmed, I promise you.*
>
> RW

James placed the letter carefully on the desk in front of him and sat thinking for a moment. 'I'd better warn the others that he suspects,' he said to himself, a rather grim smile spreading over his face. He turned to the telephone, picked up the receiver and dialled 634534 very deliberately.

A2 Read the whole text again and answer these questions with short written answers, or ask and answer them in pairs:
1 Why did James enter his house 'absent-mindedly'?
2 Why had the people at the meeting been surprised?
3 What was written on the envelope lying on the floor?
4 What did James do before he read the letter?
5 What did Ray apologise for?
6 What was Ray's excuse or explanation?
7 Why did Ray advise James not to contact the other committee members?
8 Why do you think James might be involved in the kidnapping somehow?

A3 These numbers appeared in the extract. What do they refer to?
1 1963   2 11.30   3 £10,000   4 634534

A4 Let's see again how multiple-choice items work. This time there are three choices or options in each. Study this first item, then do and discuss items 2–4.

THE STEM

> 1 James had not noticed the envelope immediately because

THE CHOICES OR OPTIONS

> **A** he was normally absent-minded.
> **B** the hallway was in darkness.
> **C** he had stepped on it when he came in.

Remember, if the stem is not already in the form of a straightforward question, try to transform it into one. The stem here ends with the word *because*, so the question is: *Why had James not noticed . . .?* And the answer is:

A? No. We are not told he was *normally* absent-minded, just that he opened the door absent-mindedly.
B? Yes. We are told 'he had stepped over it as he entered in the dark' and 'he switched on the light'.
But always check the rest of the choices or options just in case . . .!
C? No. He hadn't stepped *on* it; he had stepped *over* it. So **B** is definitely correct!

2 James opened and read the letter when   [What's the question?]
  A he was sitting in a comfortable armchair.
  B he had switched on all the lights in the house.
  C he had settled himself comfortably in his lounge.

3 The kidnapper had contacted Ray Wallace by   [What's the question?]
  A telephoning him.
  B sending him a short note.
  C asking the vicar to give him a message.

4 Ray Wallace wrote his letter on 'Vicarage' notepaper because   [What's the question?]
  A he couldn't afford any of his own.
  B he didn't want anyone to know where he was staying.
  C he had gone there to look over the churchyard.

B One of the letter types that sometimes appears in the Composition Paper 2 is a letter of apology. Often it is connected with giving advice or giving news or information about your family, school, college or work, country, etc.

B1 Here is some of the language we use in order to apologise for not doing (or having done) something, and to give advice.
Study the language carefully, then cover it and do exercise **B2**.

APOLOGISING	
Informal letter or note to a friend	Sorry I haven't written before . . . Sorry I haven't answered your last letter until now, but . . . Sorry for not writing before/not answering your last letter . . .
Neutral (to an acquaintance, for example)	I'm so/terribly sorry (that) I wasn't able to . . .
Formal letter or note to a stranger, a company, etc.	I (really) must apologise for not writing before/earlier, but . . . Please accept my (sincere) apologies for not writing before/not replying to your last letter . . .
GIVING ADVICE	
Informal/Neutral	I think/don't think (that) you ought to/should . . . If I were you, I'd/I would/I wouldn't . . . The best thing you can do is (to) / not (to) . . .
Neutral/Formal	My advice (to you) is to . . ./not to . . . You might consider [do]ing . . . (I think (that)) you would be (well) advised to . . .

B2 Rewrite these sentences beginning with the words in brackets. You might want to make some of the vocabulary more formal/informal.

Informal → Formal
1 I don't think you should tell anyone about it. (My advice . . .)
2 Sorry for not ringing you to discuss the problem. (Please accept . . .)
3 Sorry I haven't returned your book before. (I really must apologise . . .)
4 The best thing you can do is to forget the whole thing.
  (You would be . . .)

Formal → Informal
5 I think you would be well advised to reconsider the matter. (The best thing . . .)
6 I just can't apologise enough for leaving you to arrange everything.
  (Sorry . . .)
7 My advice to you is to consult a solicitor. (I think you . . .)
8 Please accept my apologies for causing you so much trouble.
  (I'm sorry . . .)

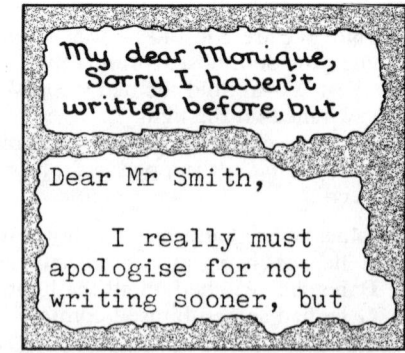

C Here is a typical First Certificate 'apology' composition. It is fairly formal, so you might add the name and address of the person you are writing to. Note where we normally write this name and address.

> 'A month ago you received a polite letter from an Australian who wrote to you on the advice of a friend of yours. The writer asked for some advice about a two-week touring holiday in your country or continent. You have only just got round to answering the letter. Write a letter to accompany some information and leaflets that you have collected.'

Write the letter, paying careful attention to the layout, and using some of the sentences, questions and prompts below to guide you.

[Name and address of the person you are writing to*]

[Your address here – but remember, **not** your name!]

Mr/Mrs/Miss/Ms [+family name],
_____,
_____

[The date here ➔ _____ 19??]

Dear Mr/Mrs/Miss/Ms _____,

    Thank you for your letter which I received _____ [When?]. I must admit that _____ [How surprised were you to hear from a total stranger?] but since [your friend's name] suggested you should write to me, I will _____ [What can you do to help?].
    First of all, however, I really must apologise _____ [For what?]. I feel _____ [Well, how do you feel?], but I know you will understand when I tell you that _____ [What's your brief explanation or excuse for not replying earlier?].
    If you are planning to come to [country/continent] for a two-week touring holiday, I would suggest that _____ [What would you suggest he/she tries to see? Where would you suggest he/she goes first? – and then where?]. I am enclosing a few _____ [What? and about what?] for you to look at.
    Please accept my sincere apologies once again _____ [For what?]. If you have time, please _____ [Invite him/her to visit you and your family]. I look forward to meeting you.

                  Yours sincerely,

                  [Sign your name here]

[*You could write the person's name and address here or, because this is not a 'business' letter, omit it completely.]

UNIT 7

How did it end?

A1 Before you read the newspaper article below, cover it and do this exercise. Imagine you are given this last sentence of a story and asked to write the story which leads up to it: 'They apologised for not being able to help more, then drove off without giving their names.' Discuss what might have led up to this last sentence.

A2 Now read the headline. What's the article going to be about? Then read the article and answer the questions in exercise **A3**.

Drama of double crash
Driver saves girl trapped underwater

by Alfred Lee

RAIN lashed down and strong winds blew as schoolteacher Miss Susan Seymour drove through the darkened outskirts of a Sussex village in her Ford Escort.

Suddenly her car hit floodwater, skidded, hurtled through a fence, rolled over twice down a bank, and crashed into a water-filled drainage ditch on its roof.

Instantly water flooded in through the broken windscreen and windows.

And 31-year-old Miss Seymour was trapped, held by her seat belt, upside down.

Water completely submerged her as she groped for her belt release. She was gulping water when she finally found it.

She did an underwater somersault. The top of her head hit the floorboard of the upturned car. Water was up to her neck.

Miss Seymour found the door handle and pushed. But it was jammed.

Five minutes passed . . . 10 minutes . . . 20 minutes . . . and all the time Miss Seymour, wearing jeans and a padded jacket which was soaked with water, was getting colder and more tired.

Her arms and legs were numb, while her neck, strained so she could keep her head above water, was aching.

Weak

Then she heard a voice from the darkness: 'Hello, are you all right?'

'Help me, please help me,' Miss Seymour shouted.

But the person could do little. He was an elderly driver who with his disabled wife had seen Miss Seymour crash.

Realising he could not help, he had continued on to find a telephone to call the police. But the location he gave for the accident was wrong. So when the couple returned to the scene – too apprehensive, too old, and too weak to get down the bank – police and ambulance were still miles away, searching for the accident. And Miss Seymour was still trapped, knowing she could hold out for only a few minutes more.

Then an amazing thing happened.

Mr Kevin Holland, also driving a Ford Escort, hit the same patch of floodwater and skidded on the verge – just 15 yards from Miss Seymour's car.

The old man called to Mr Holland: 'Quickly, there's a car in the water and a woman is trapped.'

Despite shoulder injuries, Mr Holland climbed out of his car and scrambled down the bank.

He put his arm through the window to support Miss Seymour. He realised that at all costs he had to keep her conscious.

So he talked. He asked her name, what she did, where she lived and what had happened. He told her his name, about his job as a double-glazing company manager, about his hobbies.

Rescue

And so it went on for 40 minutes, until police finally found the spot – just north of the village of Tarring Neville on the A26 between Seaford and Lewes.

Later Miss Seymour, of Bishopstone, said: 'Kevin was absolutely marvellous. I am sure I would have collapsed and drowned if he had not arrived then.'

Mr Holland, a married man, of Coldharbour Road, Upper Dicker, Sussex, said: 'Susan showed tremendous bravery.'

And the elderly couple? They apologised for not being able to help more, then drove off without giving their names.

A3

1 These questions are all about numbers – so just look for numbers.

   a How old was Miss Seymour?
   b How long was Miss Seymour in the car before she heard a voice?
   c How close to Miss Seymour's car did Mr Holland's car stop?
   d How long did Mr Holland talk to Miss Seymour before the police arrived?
   e What was the number of the road they were on when the accidents happened?

2 These are all about names – so just look for words beginning with capital letters and ignore everything else.
   IMPORTANT: the first set of questions followed the order of the events in the story. These do not.

   a What was Mr Holland's first name?
   b What was Miss Seymour's first name?
   c The accidents happened near a village. What was the name of it?
   d Where did Miss Seymour live?
   e What make of car were both Miss Seymour and Mr Holland driving?
   f What was Mr Holland's home address?

A4

Here are some statements about the order of events or actions in the story. Are the statements true or false? Look out for words like *after*, *when* and *before*, and the use of past tenses *was doing*, *had done* and *did*. Give reasons for your answers.

1 The elderly driver first arrived on the scene after Miss Seymour had crashed into the water.
2 The police arrived on the scene 40 minutes after Miss Seymour had crashed.
3 When Mr Holland arrived, Miss Seymour had just got out of her car.
4 Mr Holland had been talking to Susan for over half an hour before the police arrived.

A5

Find these words in the text. Then use the context to work out what the words mean. (Use a dictionary to check the meanings if necessary.) Ask yourself the same kinds of questions as those in the example.

Example: lashed down

What was the weather like? Was it sunny? Was it snowing? Was it raining? Was there a wind? How strong were the winds? So how was it probably raining? Just drizzling? Or pouring down, with the wind blowing it?

1 (darkened) outskirts	5 submerged	9 jammed
2 skidded	6 groped	10 numb
3 hurtled	7 gulping	11 hold out
4 flooded in	8 did a somersault	12 scrambled

UNIT 7

B Here is some more practice (see Unit 2) in joining sentences.

B1 **A series of simple actions in the past – with commas + *and***

Re-order each group of sentences below, then make one long sentence, like this:

Example: It hurtled through a fence. Suddenly her car hit floodwater. It skidded. It crashed into a ditch. It rolled over down a bank.

You write: *Suddenly her car hit floodwater, skidded, hurtled through a fence, rolled down a bank,* **and** *crashed into a ditch.*

1 He shone his torch right at me. The guard opened the door. Then he fired. He looked out. He took out his revolver. He shouted.
2 It flew out carrying a mouse in its beak. The bird hovered for a few moments. It plunged into the long grass. It caught sight of a movement below.
3 I put it into first gear. I ran to my car. I started the engine. I got in. Then I drove off as fast as I could. I closed the door.

B2 *-ing* **forms used in clauses of reason**

Complete the following sentences about the story on page 30, like this:

Realising he could not help, . . . he had continued on to find a telephone.
(= **Because he realised** he could not help. . . .)

1 Being old and weak, he . . .
2 Realising that he had to keep her conscious, . . .
3 Thinking that perhaps the driver of the second car could help, he . . .
4 Having been given the wrong location, they . . .
5 Not wanting any publicity, they . . .

C Sometimes you are given a 'starter' sentence for a story, sometimes the last sentence. In either case you will almost certainly have to *make up* a story.

C1 Here is a typical First Certificate composition with a 'starter':

> '"I knew that if he didn't see me, I had a good chance of escaping."
> Complete this story in 120–180 words.'

How might this story continue? Use the questions below to guide you.

Decision time!
Decide a who 'he' is: a guard or warden in a prison or camp? a teacher who might catch you where you shouldn't have been? or . . .?
        b where or what you wanted to 'escape' from: a prison? an unpleasant or embarrassing situation? a nextdoor neighbour? or . . .?

Paragraph 1
I knew that if he didn't see me, I had a good chance of escaping.
Where were you? behind a wall? lying in long grass? behind a door?
When had you seen 'him' (the guard?)?
What was he doing?/What did he do?

I was . . . [where?] . . .

. . . and I had seen 'the guard' as he . . . [what?] . . .

Paragraph 2
What was your best means of escape? – across the yard? over the wall? . . .
What did you do? [A number of actions]
How had you done those things? – slowly? carefully?
Was there another obstacle you had forgotten? – a locked door, for example?

I decided that . . . [what?/where?] . . .

. . . so I . . ., . . ., . . . and . . .
I had (moved) . . . [how?] . . .
. . . but there . . .

Paragraph 3
What did you do to overcome it?
How far were you now from (the guard)?
So how did you [do it]?
How long did it take?

In order to get . . ., I . . . [what?]
I was now . . . [how far?]
. . . so . . . [how?]
It only took . . . [how long?] . . .
and I was free at last! *or* I had escaped!

C2 Here is a typical 'last sentence' First Certificate composition:

What might have led up to this last sentence? You should make clear decisions (and notes) about what led up to the ending.

So – decision time again!
Decide: why your photo was in the local newspaper – did you save someone from drowning? or did someone save *you* from drowning? did you catch a large fish? or win a canoe race? or . . .? and which river was it, where and when?

Now complete this 'skeleton' of a story by answering the questions and filling in with your own ideas and details. Read the complete 'skeleton' before you begin.

> 'This is the last sentence of a story: "The next day there was a small article about it in our local newspaper, with a photo of me by the river."
> Write, in 120–180 words, the story that led up to it.'

I have only ever had my photo in a newspaper once in my life, and that was _____. [*Well, when was it? – about 10 years ago? when you were 12 years old?*] My father had just bought me my first canoe/sailing boat/ fishing rod [*Which?*] and I had gone down to our local river with a friend to do some canoeing/sailing/fishing [*Which?*].

It was a beautiful sunny day [*Or wasn't it?*] so there were lots of [*Or not many?*] other people on the river/by the river [*Which?*]. Suddenly a large motor boat went past. It annoyed everyone because _____ [*Why? Did it make so much noise? Did it upset the fish? Were the people on it having a party/making a noise? Or . . . ?*] We were watching and it was _____ [*Where?*] when we heard someone scream and someone fell off it. It was a small boy!

I didn't have time to think. I took off my _____ and _____ [*What?*], dived _____, _____, _____ and _____. [*What did you do?*] When I handed the boy to his mother, she _____. [*What did she do and/or say?*] I must admit I felt _____. [*What? very proud? embarrassed? Or . . . ?*] The next day there was a small article about it in our local newspaper, with a photo of me by the river.

UNIT 8

Can you describe the place?

A1 Here are some more items like the ones in Section A of the Reading Comprehension Paper. Here the choices are all nouns. Study the example, then do items 2–5.

> 1 The town offers visitors a wide _____ of entertainment.
> **A** kind **B** number **C** range **D** difference

Choice **C** is the correct answer. Why?

A and **B** are not used with the adjective *wide*; we would say *many kinds of* or *a large number of* (plus plural). The word *difference*, choice **D**, doesn't mean variety here, but *range*, choice **C**, does. So that's the one you want.

2 The _____ around our village is really beautiful in autumn.
  A scene **B** countryside **C** suburb **D** province

3 The factory covers _____ of about five square kilometres.
  A an area **B** a dimension **C** a measurement **D** a range

4 In the past ten years the _____ of our village has increased from 750 to 910.
  A personnel **B** people **C** population **D** neighbourhood

5 There is a helicopter service to the island from the mainland and the _____ takes 20 minutes.
  A voyage **B** way **C** passage **D** flight

A2 The three texts in this section are from a personal letter, a newspaper article and a factual brochure – **but which is which?**
Form groups of three and read one text each. Then tell the others what your text is about, where you think it comes from and why.

A

Jersey, the largest and most southerly of the Channel Islands, has an area of 45 square miles and a population approaching 80,000. It is situated in a southerly direction some 100 miles from Portland Bill on the south coast of England, but only 14 miles from the French coast of Normandy. Castles, forts and martello towers which are dotted around the coastline remind one of bygone days when invasion by the French armies was a real threat. Today's invasion comes in the more peaceful form of holidaymakers seeking the beauty of the beaches, cliffs and natural countryside. The island abounds with a good selection of restaurants and inns. The many fine shops offer a wide range of goods at VAT-free prices. The island boasts well-established tourist and farming industries, and in more recent years has become an important centre of international finance and banking.

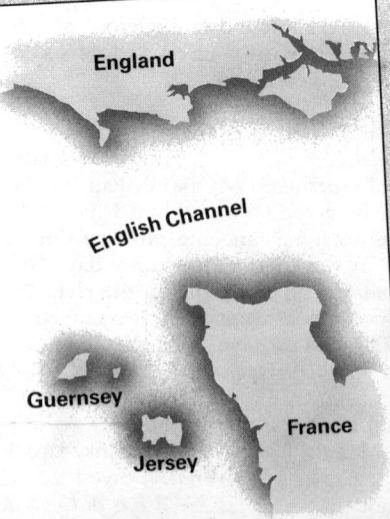

A3 Now read all three texts again. Are the following statements true or false?

1 Jersey is the ideal holiday island with no problems.
2 If you enjoy shopping, you'll enjoy a holiday in Jersey.
3 Jersey has always been a centre of international finance.
4 Tourists need a hire car on Jersey because it is so big.
5 Some people are worried about building developments on the island.
6 The brochure is more pessimistic than the newspaper article.
7 The person who wrote the letter has the same opinion as the 'regular' holidaymakers mentioned in the newspaper article.
8 Though there are plenty of restaurants on the island, eating out is expensive.

B We're having a fabulous time! The weather's gorgeous – hot and sunny – and the hotel's everything we expected it would be from the brochure. It's right near the beach at Rozel Bay so we can walk straight out of the hotel onto the sand. And the food is marvellous – much more French than English: I can't get enough crab, lobster and prawns, and they're so cheap!
The flight from London last Sunday took about 45 minutes. As soon as we landed at Jersey Airport we hired a car and had booked into our hotel and settled in within half an hour! Jersey's not a very big island, but if you ever come here, you'll find that it's a good idea to have a car. It means you can drive down to one of the beaches for the morning and then drive off and do some sightseeing in another part of the island in the afternoon.

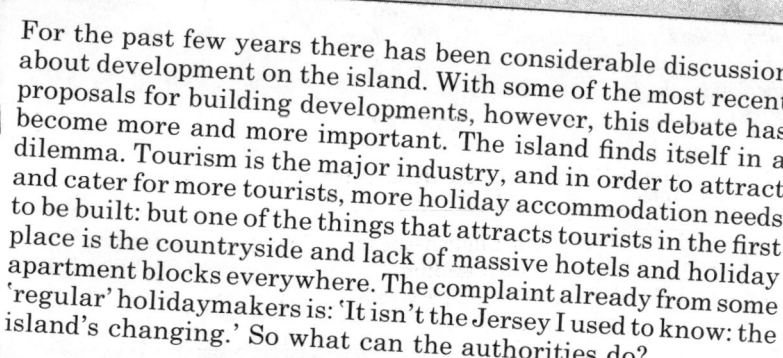

C For the past few years there has been considerable discussion about development on the island. With some of the most recent proposals for building developments, however, this debate has become more and more important. The island finds itself in a dilemma. Tourism is the major industry, and in order to attract and cater for more tourists, more holiday accommodation needs to be built: but one of the things that attracts tourists in the first place is the countryside and lack of massive hotels and holiday apartment blocks everywhere. The complaint already from some 'regular' holidaymakers is: 'It isn't the Jersey I used to know: the island's changing.' So what can the authorities do?

B1 In Unit 3, you practised writing a description of a house or apartment. Here you are going to practise writing about your home town. But first, look at this, then put *the* where necessary in the blanks in the text below.

General idea or concept (no *the*)	*Beauty* is all around us. . . . discussion about *development* on the island . . .
Specific (with *the*)	. . . *the beauty of* the beaches . . . . . . *the development* which is taking place here now . . .

(1 _____) industry is vital to the region I live in, and (2 _____) main industry is coalmining. In fact, our country not only exports (3 _____) coal abroad, but the region I live in supplies all (4 _____) coal needed by the rest of the country.

(5 _____) poverty is still a terrible problem in this country, but in particular something must be done about (6 _____) poverty you find in our large cities.

(7 _____) education must be the answer to many of our problems, but it is not only (8 _____) education of children that is important. Many adults need (9 _____) further education, too: we need as many experts in (10 _____) engineering, (11 _____) chemistry, (12 _____) banking and (13 _____) medicine as we can train.

Some people say we are making a lot of (14 _____) progress in this country, and many are amazed at (15 _____) progress we have already made in the past few years. But it isn't enough.

B2 Time to use your dictionary!

One more important point to check before you write about your own town, island, etc: think of the geography in and around your country. Then look up in a dictionary or some other reference book the places (countries, rivers, oceans, mountains, etc.) you may want to mention.
Check the English spelling and whether they need *the* or not. For example:

the Atlantic (Ocean), the Pacific (Ocean)
the Mediterranean (Sea), the Gulf of Mexico, the Caspian Sea
the (River) Nile, the Rhine
the Andes, the Himalayas; Mount Fuji, Mount Everest
the Canary Islands, the Philippines, the West Indies
Africa, Europe, Asia; Greece, France, Brazil
the Netherlands, the USA, the USSR
Rome, Lisbon, Tokyo

C1 Here is a typical First Certificate descriptive composition of this kind:

> 'Describe, as if in a letter to an English-speaking friend, the city, town or village you live in, and its surroundings.'
> (*or it might say* '. . . the town or village you have just moved to.')

The first thing to note is the phrase 'as if in a letter . . .'. In other words, you are *not* being asked to write a letter, but to imagine that what you write is *part of a letter*. So you can forget about addresses, etc.
Before you write anything, go through this questionnaire about the place you live in. Tick or fill in the boxes.

WHERE DO YOU LIVE, AND CAN YOU DESCRIBE IT?

What is it?	a city ☐ the capital ☐ a medium-sized town ☐ a village ☐
Where is it?	on or near the coast ☐ in the middle of the country ☐ in the north ☐ the south ☐ the west ☐ the east ☐
If a city, which area?	in the centre ☐ in the suburbs ☐ just outside ☐ on the outskirts ☐
If a village,	which is the nearest town/city? and how far away is it?
How would you describe it?	Is it quiet and sleepy? ☐ busy and noisy? ☐ old and picturesque? ☐ modern and lively? ☐
What is it famous for?	wine? ☐ clothes? ☐ its museums? ☐ its cathedral? ☐ what else?
What sort of area is it?	rural ☐ industrial ☐ agricultural ☐
Surrounding countryside?	flat ☐ hilly ☐ mountainous ☐
Where is it situated?	in a valley ☐ on a plain ☐ on the side of a hill ☐
What are the main industries?	
Most popular jobs:	in tourism ☐ in factories ☐ on farms ☐ what else?
Has it changed much recently?	Yes ☐ No ☐
Do you like it?	Yes ☐ No ☐ Why?/Why not?

C2 Now write the composition, using the information you have supplied in the boxes above, together with these prompts and questions.

Paragraph 1
I live in . . ., which is . . .
It is situated . . . [In which part of the country?] and is . . . kilometres from . . .
It is a [. . . describe it! . . .] and is famous for . . .

Paragraph 2
[The place] is . . . [What sort of area is it in?] and the surrounding countryside is . . .
There are a lot of . . . near [the place] and visitors often . . .

Paragraph 3
The main industries of the area/ in [the place] are . . . and most of the people there are employed in . . .
My father/cousins/brothers, for example, work . . .

Paragraph 4
In the past [ten] years, [the place] [. . . has it changed much or not? . . .], but/so [. . . Do people still live in the way they used to, or have people started to . . .?].
I . . . [Do you like it or not? Did you like it more [ten] years ago?]

UNIT 9

What can I say?

A1 Imagine you have just won an Oscar, the award for Best Actor or Best Actress, at this year's Hollywood ceremony. What would you say? Make a few notes for your 'thank you speech', then compare them with a partner's.

A2 Read this extract from a popular romantic novel. See how similar the speech in it is to what you had planned. Then do the exercises that follow.

'AND finally tonight, will you please welcome the winner of this year's other top award, the very highest accolade our profession has to offer. Actress of the Year for the second year running, for her role in 'Flying High', in which . . .'

Sophie had risen to her feet as in a trance and was already squeezing between the tables when her name was announced. She caught a glimpse of Peggy to her left, head bowed and shoulders gently shaking. Her mind was still racing as she climbed the steps to the stage and passed along the line of grinning celebrities and mumbled clichés. 'Many congratulations . . . You deserve it . . . Wonderful achievement . . . Well done . . . Marvellous.'

She moved to the microphone, clearing her throat as the applause died down. She looked briefly again towards Peggy's table, but her eyes were still lowered. Was there to be no reconciliation?

'I'd like to say first how honoured I am to have been presented with this truly magnificent award. It does make me feel very humble, I assure you.'

She realised she sounded like every other award-winner that evening, but the platitudes continued.

'A film is always a joint effort, with literally hundreds of people contributing. The list is too long for me to mention everybody, but I'd like to take this opportunity of thanking a few very special individuals. I owe a lot to our producer, Harry Silverman, who got everything off the ground and was always there with a sympathetic ear when needed.'

'I also want to say a personal thank you to my agent, Joe Harper, who first interested me in the project and overcame my initial reluctance. And of course, on behalf of everyone associated with the film, can I express my . . . our appreciation to our director, John J. Prestenburger, without whom the film would never have been made. Or if it had been, not half as well.'

She paused, feeling she had finished, but then found herself continuing.

'I'd also just like to express my . . .' Gratitude was not the word. Neither was affection. '. . . express my respect for Peggy Byrne, who played the part of Angie's mother with so much . . .'

She was saved by a burst of applause.

'I think if I had been one of the judges tonight, she would have been standing here in my place.'

As she spoke the words, she realised that she really meant them. Her gaze went once more in Peggy's direction. Their eyes met. Sophie thought she detected a slight nod and even the trace of a smile on the other's face. A gesture of friendship at last?

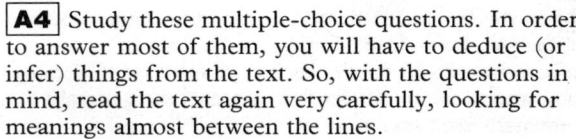

A3 To help you with some of the new vocabulary in the text, find words which match these definitions:

1 recognition of talent; an honour
2 a semi-conscious state
3 a brief sight
4 unimportant, modest
5 flat, dull remarks; clichés
6 co-operative; shared
7 unwillingness or opposition
8 a small sign or indication

A4 Study these multiple-choice questions. In order to answer most of them, you will have to deduce (or infer) things from the text. So, with the questions in mind, read the text again very carefully, looking for meanings almost between the lines.

1 What was Sophie doing when her name was announced?
  A Looking at Peggy.
  B Sitting at a table.
  C Walking towards the stage.
  D Trembling with excitement.

2 Why was Peggy's head bowed?
  A She was coughing.
  B She was most probably very disappointed.
  C She didn't want people to see her laughing.
  D She couldn't stand the people on her table.

3 The opening lines of Sophie's speech consisted of
  A a number of entertaining comments.
  B one or two old jokes.
  C a series of unoriginal remarks.
  D some rather arrogant statements.

4 Who persuaded Sophie to take part in the film?
  A Harry Silverman.
  B Joe Harper.
  C John J. Prestenburger.
  D Peggy Byrne.

5 Sophie genuinely believed that Peggy
  A hated her.
  B was enjoying the evening.
  C agreed with her.
  D should have won the award.

6 What was the relationship between Sophie and Peggy?
  A They were rivals appearing in different films.
  B They were actresses in the same film.
  C They were mother and daughter.
  D They were very good friends.

UNIT 9

B In the First Certificate Composition Paper you may be asked to write a 'speech'. It might be a speech of welcome, or introducing a guest to an audience; it might be a speech of thanks, or of goodbye, or of congratulation. Whatever the message, we generally use quite emphatic language when we are speaking in public and we sometimes exaggerate the facts and our feelings.

B1 Study the different ways in which we can do this, and say what the 'ordinary' word, phrase or sentence would be to replace those on the right.

a	choosing strong adjectives:	magnificent / wonderful / marvellous
b	adding an adjective to strengthen a noun:	sincere appreciation / deep regret / heartfelt thanks
c	using superlative forms:	the very highest accolade / one of the finest films of all time
d	using 'intensifying' adverbs:	truly magnificent / absolutely marvellous
e	strengthening comparative forms:	not half as well / nowhere near as good / not nearly as talented
f	stressing auxiliary verbs:	He *must* be the best singer in the competition.
g	adding *do / does / did* for emphasis:	It *does* make me feel very humble. I *did* enjoy your performance.

B2 Emphasise or exaggerate the simple statements as in these examples:

> It was a good meal. ⟶ It was an absolutely delicious meal!
>
> He's a good player. ⟶ He *must* be one of the most talented players in the game today.

1 Thank you for a nice evening.
2 This is a happy day for me.
3 He has been a very good friend to me for some time.
4 I think she's a good actress.
5 I'd like to say I'm sorry.
6 I'm not as clever or as talented as our next guest on the show.

B3 During a speech of welcome or introduction, for example, you may need to summarise a person's career, list his or her achievements, etc. Let's look at one way of doing this.

> *Before starting* his writing career, our guest was more interested in radio. (= Before he started . . .)
> *After leaving* college, he worked for some years in the BBC studios. (= After he left . . .)
> *While working* for Radio 4, he decided to try and write a novel. (= While he was working . . .)
> *Since completing* that first novel, he has written twenty books. (= Since he completed . . .)

Using the structures above, make sentences from the following prompts. Note that you will have to arrange each set into a logical sequence.

1 (*You are welcoming Sheila Bloom, a well-known actress, to your school*)
play 'Juliet' on the London stage / be discovered by a Hollywood producer
meet that producer / make ten films and win dozens of awards
become an actress / want to be a singer
leave Drama School / work in the theatre for some years

40

UNIT 9

2 (*You are saying goodbye to old Mr Smith, who is retiring from the company*)
come to work here / have a number of positions in the company
work here for 40 years / become assistant manager five years ago
come to this company / work as a teacher in a language school
work there / learn a lot about people

C1 Here is a typical First Certificate composition of the 'speech' kind:

> 'Your English teacher is leaving after teaching your class and others for five years. You have been asked to give a short farewell speech on behalf of parents, staff and pupils on your teacher's last day at work. Write what you would say.'

Read through this speech, noting the suggested alternatives and thinking how you would fill in the blanks (_____). (This is *not* a multiple-choice exercise: the pairs or groups of phrases, separated by a '/', are equally good alternatives.)

> Ladies and gentlemen, and fellow pupils/students!
>
> As you all know, today we are saying goodbye to / losing Mr Harper, who is leaving to start work in _____ / to become Director of _____. I'm sure we all congratulate him on his appointment / his promotion, but at the same time we are extremely sorry to see him go / to lose him.
>
> Mr Harper will be remembered here as a first-class / an excellent teacher, whose lessons have always been _____, never _____.
>
> While working here, he has done a great deal for the school / been a most popular member of staff, and has helped hundreds of pupils / students to pass the First Certificate / learn to speak and write English / understand English grammar better. Since joining the school, he has contributed an enormous amount both inside and outside the classroom / to all aspects of school life.
>
> Many of us are grateful to him for his help with the sports club / enthusiastic participation in our film society and his interest in our excursion programme / work with the older boys and girls. In short, he will be sadly missed.
>
> On behalf of everybody here, I'd like to wish him / may I wish him success / all the best in the future / in his new position, and as a token of our thanks / gratitude / appreciation, I have great pleasure in presenting you, sir, with this _____. We hope it will remind you of five happy years spent at _____.

C2 Now adapt the above as necessary to write a speech of 120–180 words saying goodbye to the Secretary who is retiring after twenty years at your school or college.

UNIT 10

What are the pros and cons?

A1 Items in Section A of the Reading Comprehension Paper quite often test your knowledge of prepositions. Study and discuss the example, then do items 2–5.

> 1 One argument in favour _____ the plan is that it will bring work to the area.
> **A** for **B** of **C** to **D** at
>
> Choice **B** is the correct answer. Why?

2 The Chairman presented three clear options _____ the Committee.
   A before **B** at **C** to **D** with

3 These goods will have to be transported _____ sea.
   A at **B** on **C** by **D** through

4 One of the arguments _____ the scheme is the enormous cost.
   A of **B** to **C** about **D** against

5 'We have decided that Plan 3 is the most practical and least expensive,' the Chairman said. 'We shall therefore _____ with that Plan.'
   A proceed **B** adopt **C** change **D** follow

A2 Read the text below to find answers to these questions:
1 When did BP start producing oil at Wytch Farm?
2 When did BP apply to the Council for permission to develop the oilfield?
3 What was the major problem, and what were the 'options'?
4 Did BP decide on its own that a new pipeline to Hamble was the best solution?
5 Why was the route for a new pipeline chosen carefully?

The international petroleum company BP has been producing oil at the Wytch Farm oilfield on the South Coast of England since 1979. In July 1984 BP announced plans to develop the oilfield from the existing production level of 4,500 barrels a day up to 60,000 barrels a day. Unprecedented consultation on all elements of the development proposal took place, leading to major changes in BP's original plan. In March 1986 applications were submitted to the Dorset County Council to develop the oilfield and in October of that year permission was granted. However, there was one major problem – how to transport the increased amount of oil away from the Wytch Farm area. These were the main options [see map opposite]:
   1 By rail through an expanded Furzebrook terminal.
   2 By pipeline to a deep water terminal in Portland Harbour.
   3 By pipeline to an existing oil terminal at Hamble on Southampton Water.
   4 By pipeline to a new tanker terminal in Poole Harbour.
After very wide consultation BP felt that a new pipeline to Southampton Water would be the best solution and therefore proposed a pipeline route to an existing terminal at Hamble. The route was carefully chosen to avoid residential areas and amenity areas as far as possible. It also avoided ecologically sensitive areas, listed buildings and scheduled ancient monuments. In December 1986 a public enquiry was held into the route and in July 1987 the Secretary of State for Energy found in BP's favour and gave permission for the Wytch Farm-to-Hamble pipeline. Construction on the project began soon afterwards and is expected to take about two years.

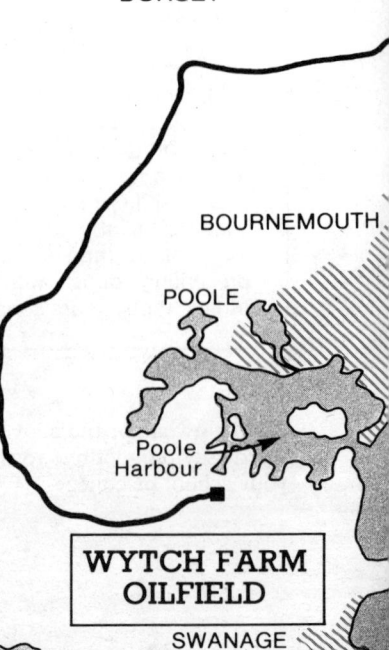

UNIT 10

A3 The two texts below were written while the 'options' debate was going on. Work in pairs and each read one of them silently. Then tell each other

1 where you think it was taken from (and give a reason);
2 which option was thought best, and why.
3 what other valuable or interesting information the text gave; and
4 whether you personally agree with the option, and give reasons.

a
Underground route, not by rail

Moves to transport thousands of barrels of Wytch Farm oil by rail are on the wrong track, claims Hurn parish council.

It decided it would be better to stop pollution by building an underground pipeline through the New Forest to Fawley rather than start a rail link that would create jobs.

Chairman Cllr. Alan Whipp and his colleagues were concerned that rail transport could not guarantee against pollution in Portland and Poole Harbour.

'We have experienced gas pipelines running through the Avon Valley, Sopley and Ripley, and the grass, crops and hedgerows have grown back over them. There seems no danger of pollution and the countryside is unscarred,' he said.

Members favoured the pipeline after considering the four transport options that BP had presented to Christchurch policy committee.

(27th September)

b
Rail oil – outsider's view

Sir – I refer to recent items about the Wytch Farm oil deposits. As an 'outsider', but one who has spent many happy holidays in Poole, Bournemouth and Swanage areas, I hope you will not mind if I comment.

I am delighted that oil has been found from a national point of view, but worry about its transport. I'm most puzzled by the virulent anti-rail bias that seems to have sprung up in Poole/Bournemouth. I have lived near railway lines that are much busier than any will ever be in Poole and area. I can assure people who are concerned that the daytime operations which are planned by British Rail to transport the oil will hardly be noticed.

My family and I travel into your area by rail and would certainly not come if rail to Poole and to Wareham was not available. The additional oil trains will ensure 20 years or more continued development of the railway west of Bournemouth.

(19th November)

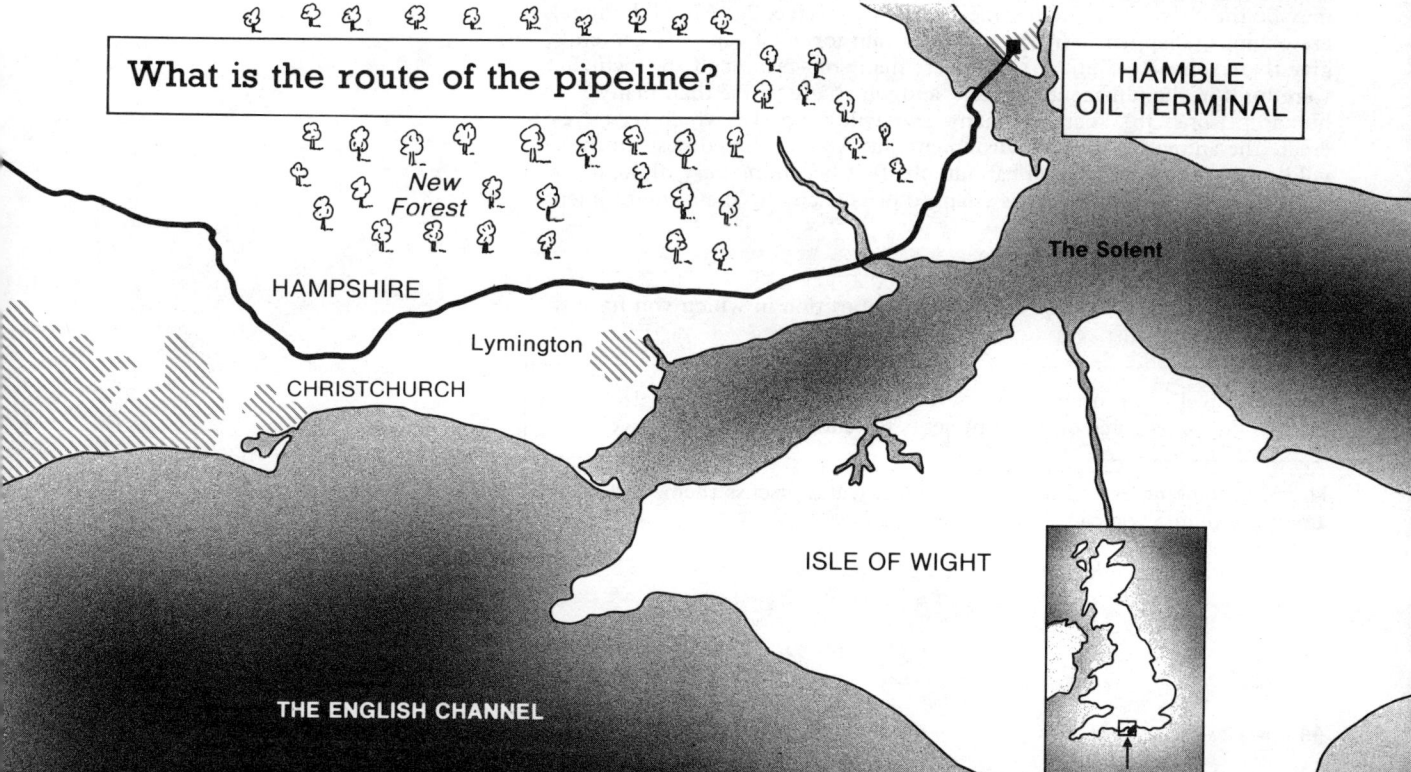

UNIT 10

B Remember that one of the composition types you can choose in the First Certificate is a discursive composition or 'argument'. In Unit 5 there is practice in arguing for *or* against an idea or a proposal. Here you are going to practise putting the arguments for *and* against, or expressing the pros *and* cons, the advantages *and* disadvantages.
What kind of language might you need to write a composition like this?

B1 One thing you will almost certainly want to do is to contrast ideas. Study these ways of contrasting ideas, then do the exercise below.

One of the (most important) arguments in favour of long school holidays is that it gives students a rest, *but* we must/should not forget that *an (equally) important argument against* them is that they disrupt students' learning.

On the one hand long school holidays give students a rest,
but on the other (hand)
On the other hand, however, } they disrupt students' learning.

Although/Though/While
Despite the fact that } long school holidays may be a good idea,
nevertheless/(un)fortunately they disrupt students' learning.

Rewrite the following paragraph by joining each pair of sentences (1a and 1b, 2a and 2b, etc.) using the sentence types above as appropriate. The passage is about the pros and cons of keeping wild animals in captivity.

1a) Many people agree that no animals should be kept in captivity. 1b) It may be the only way to help some species to survive. 2a) All wild animals are obviously happier living free. 2b) Certain forms of captivity can still give them some freedom. 3a) There are many old-fashioned zoos which were built in the nineteenth century and which are worse than many human prisons. 3b) There are many new 'wildlife parks' which try to re-create the animals' natural environment. 4a) Animals breed best 'in the wild' or in their own natural habitat. 4b) It is becoming very difficult for some animals because Man has changed or is changing their environment in so many different ways.

C1 Here is a typical First Certificate composition in which you have to argue for *and* against.

'Space travel – is it useful or wasteful? Write between 120 and 180 words outlining some of the arguments for and against space travel.'

Here are some notes you might make. Study and discuss them, and add any more points you can think of *for* or *against*:

For (= Space travel is useful)
1. Man – conquered Earth – now time – look at space.
2. Increases knowledge of universe, Earth – and our origins?
3. Bonuses for medicine, weather-forecasting, communications, etc.
4. Future – people emigrate to other planets – solve Earth population problem?

Against (= Space travel is wasteful)
1. Enormous cost – $ millions to send one/two men into space.
2. Manned space flight – up to now (1988) only reached Moon.
3. Only unmanned flights to nearest planets (e.g. Mars) – how much to send men?
4. Vital problems on Earth: overpopulation, hunger, disease, poverty – all need money. Use money to try to solve these problems.

C2 Even if you don't use all the points above in your composition, there are two ways in which you could write the arguments. This is the first way you could write the composition. Read it carefully and notice the kind of language used.

One paragraph listing all the arguments *for*...

One of the most important arguments in favour of space travel is that it is in man's nature to discover and explore new places. Now that we have conquered Earth, the oceans and space are the only real challenges left. A second reason for continuing present programmes is the enormous help they can give us in terms of medical research, communications and weather-forecasting. And then there are also the benefits future generations may enjoy. Who knows, perhaps Space holds the answer to our present population and pollution problems.

...and one listing all the arguments *against*

On the other side of the argument, however, one of the great disadvantages is the huge cost of all space exploration. Many would say that the billions of dollars spent on sending just a few men around the Earth and to the moon has been a complete waste of money. They argue that we have many problems here on this planet and that those billions are needed to solve them. The fact that in future even more money would be needed for space programmes is also an argument against them.

C3 You could also write the same composition *as a series of paragraphs in which you constantly compare **for** and **against***.
Write the same composition as the one above, but this time constantly comparing *for* and *against*. Use some of these sentence patterns:

– One of the most important arguments in favour of space travel is . . ., but we must not forget that . . . .
– On the one hand . . ., but on the other hand . . .
– One of the great advantages of space travel is . . ., but at the same time there is also a major disadvantage, and that is that . . .
– While space travel/space exploration may be a good idea, nevertheless . . .
– Despite the fact that space travel . . ., (un)fortunately . . .
– Although the exploration of space . . ., nevertheless . . .

C4 Now try composition 10 on page 86.

UNIT 11

Could you tell me about it?

A1 Work in pairs. One of you look over text 1 and the other look over text 2 for about 20 seconds. Then tell your partner as much as you can about it.

1. Travel and Tourism Courses in Canada

WHY CANADA? This vast and varied country with one of the highest standards of living in the world has succeeded in marrying American technology with institutions and culture based on European models. It is not for nothing that Canadians call us their European 'cousins'.

WHY TRAVEL AND TOURISM? This is one of the most important growth industries in the world and English is undeniably the main means of communication inside it.

WHY OTTVAN COLLEGE OF TOURISM? Established in 1956 as part of the Camden Foundation, a non-profit-making trust, the College enjoys a worldwide reputation for its English for Special Purposes courses. It offers the opportunity of studying the language in a friendly but serious atmosphere while following a full training course in all aspects of the hospitality industry.

Notable among our facilities are a multi-media learning centre, video studios, and a fully equipped library.

COURSE CONTENT Participants may expect to cover these subjects during their course:
– tour operations – communications – selling skills and customer relations – cashiering and banking – basic financial administration – basic international law – air, sea, rail and road travel.

We lay emphasis on active participation by students in a wide variety of different activities ranging from role-plays, simulations and video work to text analysis and research projects.

COURSE DATES Four-week courses begin on the first Monday of every month.

ACCOMMODATION Over the years we have established a nationwide network of first-class welcoming host families.

FEES We have a special grant-assisted fee structure. For further details and enrolment form, please apply to: Ottvan College of Tourism, Ottowa PO Box XYZ

2. Far and away your best choice NEW ZEALAND!

6-week courses   incredible value   Auckland Academy founded in 1979

Here's your chance to discover the real New Zealand, the little-known country that's got the lot! Stunning scenery, fabulous beaches, breathtaking mountains. Experience for yourself the mysteries of our thermal springs, volcanic plateaux, rivers, lakes and rich pine forests.

While you're here, kill two birds with one stone and take a useful course in the exciting and challenging hospitality industry. Look at what you get at the Auckland Academy of Travel and Tourism:

– full English programme every morning
– a choice of specialist options including courses in Hotel Reception, Food Service and Hotel Operations. (Subjects like welcoming guests, presentation of bills and simple accounting are covered.)
– accommodation in a student hostel or self-catering apartment
– full programme of leisure and recreational activities: barbecues, international meals evenings, half-day and weekend excursions to Lake Rotoruo and its famous springs, spectacular Waitomo cave and Waipoua forest and its giant kauri tree.

If you want to know more about what we do, our prices and the special sponsorship we can arrange (some pay as little as £150 p.w.), write to: The Director, Auckland Academy, Auckland, New Zealand

A2 Read both texts a little more carefully now, compare them and answer the questions below. (Tick the boxes in the columns.) Still try to read quickly and remember, you don't have to read every word to get the information you want.

According to the adverts,
which of the centres

	C	NZ
1 has the more varied social programme?		✓
2 has been in existence the longer?	✓	
3 is not a commercial enterprise?	✓	
4 has the shorter courses?	✓	
5 offers accommodation where you look after yourself?		✓
6 has impressive equipment?	✓	
7 allows students to choose what they study?		✓
8 offers the broader look at tourism?		

C = Canada   NZ = New Zealand

What have you noticed so far about the different styles of the two advertisements?

A3 Answer these multiple-choice questions about the texts.

1 Canada is described as being
  A a wealthy country.
  B more like America than Europe.
  C a growing nation.
  D European in its attitude to technology.

2 In the New Zealand advertisement, 'killing two birds with one stone' refers to
  A being excited and challenged.
  B taking courses in tourism and travel.
  C seeing the country and doing a course.
  D opportunities for hunting and fishing.

3 What do both centres have in common?
  A They stress the importance of a leisure programme.
  B They arrange trips by road, rail and sea.
  C They realise the importance of technology.
  D They can arrange a reduction in the fees to be paid.

A4 Which of the two places (Canada or New Zealand) would you like to go to? Why?

B1 Here are two letters of reply to the advertisements on page 46. Read them and then discuss in small groups how they are different. (For example, is one more formal than the other? If so, how?)

Dear Sirs,

I saw an advert in a paper recently (I can't remember which) about hotel courses in New Zealand. It sounded great and I think I'd be very interested. Provided, of course, that the price was right. How much does it all cost? If you include the return flight from Rome, that is. Have you got any brochures you could send me perhaps?

Hope to hear from you.
        Yours,

        . . . .

Dear Sir or Madam,

I was very interested to read your advertisement in the November issue of 'Global Tourists' for four-week courses in Travel and Tourism.

I would be extremely grateful if you could send me further details regarding the course content and more information about accommodation arrangements. Do you think you could also let me know exactly how much a course would cost and whether the cost of travelling to and from Canada is included in the grant-assisted scheme which your advertisement referred to.

There was no mention in your advertisement of any social or leisure activities. Could you please send me such a programme if you have one?

I look forward to hearing from you.
        Yours faithfully,

        . . . .

B2 In the examination, you may be asked to write a semi-formal letter to a company or some other organisation. For this it is better to imitate the style of the second letter above. (For notes on the layout, beginnings and endings of letters, see Units 1 and 6, pages 8–9 and 29.)

Here are some pairs of phrases. Decide in each case which is more formal.

1 I'd like to know if . . .   Could I enquire whether . . .?
2 . . . get in touch as soon as you can.   . . . contact me at your earliest convenience.
3 . . . further details regarding . . .   . . . more information about . . .
4 I look forward to hearing from you in the near future. Write when you can.
5 Thanks a lot in advance.   Thanking you in anticipation.
6 I would be grateful if you could let me have . . .   Can you send me . . .?
7 Could you write back soon?   An early reply would be appreciated.
8 You didn't say anything about . . .   You did not refer to . . .

Now cover each column in turn and try to remember the 'equivalent' phrase.

B3 When we want to have something explained or clarified, we often start a sentence with a *what*-clause, like this:

What I would really like to know is	whether / what / why ...
What I am really interested in is	when / which / whose ...
What I did not understand was	who / how / how long ...
What I would like you to explain is	how much / how many ...

Look back at the two advertisements on page 46 and write at least eight sentences like this. Ask for clarification of things you would like to know more about.

C1 Read this letter carefully, noting the layout, style and content. Then use it as a model to write a similar one to the Tourist Information Centre of an English-speaking country which you have always wanted to visit.

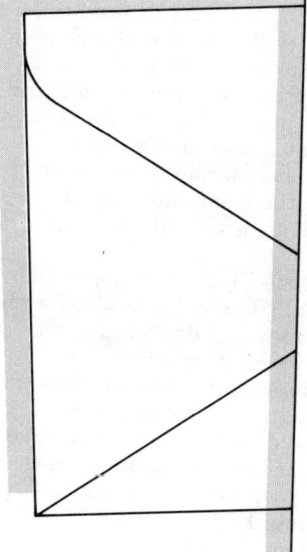

```
                                          244, Peking Road,
                                          Quarry Bay,
British Tourist Authority,                HONG KONG
Thames Tower,
Black's Road,
Hammersmith,
London  W6 9EL              24th January 1988

Dear Sir or Madam,

    I am planning to take a three-week touring holiday
in Britain with my wife and two teenage children this
coming May. We shall be arriving at Heathrow Airport
on 2nd May and, after spending a few nights in London,
would like to see as much of the country as possible.
    I would be very grateful if you could send me some
brochures and any other relevant information you have
regarding prices, accommodation and car hire facilities.
What we are really keen to see is the sort of place
that few tourists go to, unspoilt villages, smallish
towns and one or two large industrial cities. Perhaps
I could ask you to suggest a route which would give
us a general impression of both rural and urban England.
    As this will be our first time in Europe, we should
also like to spend some time on the Continent. Could you
let us have details about weekend visits from London to
other European cities such as Paris and Amsterdam.
    Thanking you in anticipation for your help.

                              Yours faithfully,

                                R. Hue

                              R. Hue
```

C2 Now plan and write composition 11 on page 87.

UNIT 12

What did you do next?

A1

1 Have you had a day recently when everything seemed to go wrong? Tell a partner or the class about it.
2 Form small groups and tell each other about times in your life when you felt very embarrassed and wanted to disappear into a hole in the ground.

A2 The text below is about how things went wrong when an artist was asked to go and paint the portrait of an important military man at the man's home. What things do you think could go wrong in a situation like that? Make a list.

A3 Now read the story and see how many of your ideas were right.

I had been commissioned to paint a portrait of the newly-appointed Chief of Defence Staff. Since there was to be a domestic background in the picture, the first two sittings were to be held in his home rather than in my studio.

I arrived and laid out my equipment happily, and we tried out his chair in various positions in different lights. My first error was when, trying to be helpful, I attempted to pass his Field Marshal's baton to him (delicate gold filigree top, velvet-covered, presented to him by the Queen just two weeks before). Somehow I missed – and it dropped with an echoing thwang into a tin wastepaper bin. That, not surprisingly, did not go down very well.

Determined to prove that painters are not really clumsy idiots, I set to work – deliberately painting with deft, rhythmic arm movements. But I knew, as that fully-loaded brush sprang out of my hand and hurtled like a rocket across his drawing room, that it was going to touch down on the one bit of the Aubusson carpet, in the far corner, that I had not protected with dust-sheets ... and Alazarin Crimson, just right for painting the ribbon of the Order of the Bath, is unfortunately so powerful a colour that it is virtually impossible to remove the stain completely.

We had to stop for twenty minutes whilst I did what I could to put right the damage with my turpentine and his detergent. Before starting again, I asked if I might wash my hands. The Field Marshal was obviously only too glad to be rid of me for a bit, and directed me to the little cloakroom by the front door.

While there, I thought I would take the opportunity first to spend a penny; as I washed my hands, though, I became aware that the loo was making the strangest noises. I went across to have a look at it and, incapable of action, I watched as the water-level gurgled over the brim and several gallons were deposited all over the floor.

The next time I had a sitting at the Field Marshal's home, I was filled with good resolutions as I drove up to the front door. He, looking slightly strained I thought, greeted me there. He was, though, still surprisingly courteous: holding the door wide open for me as I carried my portable easel through, he gave me a weak smile. 'Good morning, Field Marshal!' I beamed, as I eased past him with a caricature of extreme care. Then the collapsible leg on the easel fell open, and removed a large chunk of the door.

A4 Now answer these multiple-choice questions about the story.

1 Why was the early painting work not done in a studio?
   A The Chief of Defence was newly-appointed.
   B The artist had too much equipment.
   C The sitting was going to be a long one.
   D The picture was going to have a home setting.

2 When did the first accident occur?
   A As soon as the artist arrived.
   B Just before the artist started painting.
   C After the painting had been started.
   D Two weeks before the sitting.

3 What happened to the artist's brush in the second incident?
   A It just dropped out of his hand.
   B It landed in a bin.
   C It fell onto a dust-sheet.
   D It travelled some distance.

4 What did the artist do during the twenty-minute break?
   A He tried to remove the paint stain.
   B He took a well-earned rest.
   C He mended the damaged paintbrush.
   D He spent a lot of time in the cloakroom.

5 What do we learn about the incident in the cloakroom?
   A It was not the artist's fault.
   B It wouldn't cost a penny to put right.
   C It was a result of the artist washing his hands.
   D It happened because the toilet made funny noises.

6 What happened on the artist's next visit?
   A He crashed his car into the Field Marshal's house.
   B The Field Marshal was extremely rude to the artist.
   C There was another accident in the house.
   D The Field Marshal felt much better.

UNIT 12

B1 In the examination you may have to write a composition about a dramatic event in your life. If you like, you can write about something that really happened to you.

Or – and this is sometimes easier – you can invent a story.

In this exercise we have given you one short story and the prompts for two more. Write the two stories, using the same sentence patterns as in the model.

MODEL STORY **Disastrous party situation**	**STORY 1** **Road accident situation**	**STORY 2** **Eventful babysitting situation**
First paragraph: Before the event(s)		
Some time ago I was invited to a party by some distant friends. I was looking forward to it, so I got there early. From then on, everything went wrong.	About six months ago / I – invited to visit friends in country. I – look forward to it / set out early. From then on, everything went wrong.	A couple of years ago / I – asked to babysit for friends of my parents. They / put children to bed when I arrived / I / quite happy. But from then on, everything went wrong.
Middle one or two paragraphs: The event(s)		
For a start, I had just arrived at the party when my hostess offered me a drink. Just as she was handing it to me, I coughed and the wine went all over her dress.	I – turn into main road / crash into another car	I – turn on the TV / the five-year-old wake up
	I / reverse / cyclist – come along / ride into the side of car	I – tell her a short story / the baby – wake up / start crying
As if that wasn't enough, as soon as I saw what had happened, I stood up and knocked the glass out of her hand. The glass broke and the rest of the wine went over the carpet. And to cap it all, I had no sooner bent down to pick up the pieces than someone carrying a fruit salad came in and fell over me.	As if that wasn't enough, – / get out of the car / motorcyclist ran into my car door	As if that wasn't enough, I – pick her up / the six-year-old get up / go to bathroom She/spill shampoo all over floor
	And finally, to cap it all, I / start to cross the road to help the cyclist / taxi – knock me down	And then to cap it all, I / clean the bathroom / the baby – want to be changed
Last paragraph: After the event(s)		
My hostess didn't speak to me again until I had promised to pay for all the damage. While I was saving up to pay her back, I promised myself I would never drink wine at a party again.	I / not move again much / they – take my leg out of plaster	They – not go back to sleep / the film on TV finish
	I – lie in hospital / promise – sell my car as soon as possible	I – sit on bus on way home / promise – never go out babysitting again

B2 When you write a story, you might often want to write what people say. Look at the two ways you could write what the artist and the Field Marshal said to each other – with direct speech or reported speech:

'Can you come on Monday?' the Field Marshal asked the artist. →	The Field Marshal asked the artist if he could come on Monday.
'The Queen gave me this baton two weeks ago,' said the officer. →	The officer said (that) the Queen had given him the baton two weeks before.
The artist said to the Field Marshal: 'I'm ready to begin.' →	The artist told the Field Marshal (that) he was ready to begin.

Report the following as in the examples above:

1 'I think the picture is going very well,' said the artist.
2 'There's some detergent in the kitchen,' the officer said to the painter.
3 'I'll soon get rid of this stain,' said the painter.
4 'May I wash my hands?' asked the artist.
5 'Where's the cloakroom, please?' he asked the Field Marshal.
6 'Do you know how much that carpet cost?' the officer asked the artist.
7 'I'm sorry about what happened,' the painter said to the Field Marshal.
8 'I'm sure things will go better tomorrow,' he said.
9 'Can I pass you your baton, Field Marshal?' the artist said.
10 'I'm looking forward very much to seeing the final result,' he said.

C Now read the story on page 50 quickly again and write a composition about what happened from the Field Marshal's point of view. These prompts are to help you to structure the composition and to use a variety of sentence patterns.

Paragraph 1
I had just been appointed Chief of Defence Staff. I thought . . . [What? that it would be a good idea to . . .] [So what did you do? Who did you contact?]

Paragraph 2
As soon as he arrived . . . [Did you know it would be a disaster? Did you feel that something was wrong?] He had no sooner . . . [What? unpacked his things? laid out his brushes?] . . . than . . . [What?] [And what did you say to him at that point?]

Paragraph 3
[Then what happened while he was painting?] [Where did the brush land?] [How did you feel? But did you show your feelings?] [How did you feel when he left the room? How long did you have to wait?] [What did you hear while he was in the bathroom?] [What did you do as soon as you heard the noise?] [What did you find?] [What did you tell him?]

Paragraph 4
[How did you feel the next time, when he came for your second sitting?] He had no sooner . . . than . . . [What happened to the easel? and to the door?] [What did you promise yourself after this experience? – that you would never . . .]

UNIT 13

What do they look like?

A1 Imagine you are going to an English-speaking country and that someone is going to meet you when you arrive. How would you describe yourself so that the person can recognise you in a crowd?

A2 In the following passage, the writer describes a small group of people. Read it, then say which (one or more) of the people is or are not described physically.

> A glance at his drawing-room when Valentin entered it was enough to make certain that his principal guest was not there, at any rate. He saw all the other pillars of the little party: he saw Lord Galloway, the English Ambassador – a choleric old man with a russet face like an apple, wearing the blue ribbon of the Garter. He saw Lady Galloway, slim and thread-like, with silver hair and a face sensitive and superior. He saw her daughter, Lady Margaret Graham, a pale and pretty girl with an elfish face and copper-coloured hair. He saw the Duchess of Mont St Michel, black-eyed and opulent, and with her her two daughters, black-eyed and opulent also. He saw Dr Simon, a typical French scientist, with glasses, a pointed brown beard, and a forehead barred with wrinkles which come through constantly elevating the eyebrows. He saw Father Brown of Cobhole, in Essex, whom he had recently met in England. He saw – perhaps with more interest than any of those – a tall man in uniform, who had bowed to the Galloways without receiving any very hearty acknowledgement, and who now advanced alone to pay his respects to his host. This was Commandant O'Brien, of the French Foreign Legion. He was a slim yet somewhat swaggering figure, clean-shaven, dark-haired, and blue-eyed, and as seemed natural in an officer of that famous regiment of victorious failures and successful suicides, he had an air at once dashing and melancholy. He was by birth an Irish gentleman, and in boyhood had known the Galloways – especially Margaret Graham. He had left his country after some crash of debts, and now expressed his complete freedom from British etiquette by swinging about in uniform sabre and spurs. When he bowed to the Ambassador's family, Lord and Lady Galloway bent stiffly, and Lady Margaret looked away.

A3 **Who's Who?** Read the passage again to find out which of the people

1 had black eyes.
2 was (or were) clean-shaven.
3 was (or were) noticeably slim.
4 had a beard.
5 had dark or black hair.
6 had blue eyes.
7 had a pale complexion.
8 had a red face.

Make sentences with these prompts, choosing from the structures given:

1 extremely handsome / great charm
2 somewhat plump / extremely graceful dancer
3 still in his twenties / nearly bald
4 slightly cruel eyes / a rather mean mouth
5 quite good-looking / reasonably charming
6 Scandinavian / surprisingly dark-skinned
7 at least fifty years old / still very athletic
8 fairly well-built / pretty weak physically

C1 Read this 'Wanted' poster carefully. Imagine you were a witness to the armed robbery in Hightown on that Saturday and the police description of the man was taken from a written statement that you made. Write that statement.
Note: Don't simply write a series of short sentences with *He was . . .* or *He had . . .*: try to use some of the language you have practised in the Unit to join ideas (e.g. *As well as . . ., Although . . .,* etc.) and use phrases such as *As far as I can remember, . . ., I couldn't see very clearly, but . . ., I noticed [his hair] particularly because . . .,* and so on.

C2 For fun, write a similar 'Wanted' poster for a member of your class. When you have finished, read it out and see if the other members of the class can identify the wanted person.

C3 Below is a photograph of an athletics club you once belonged to. You found the photo a few days ago and are now sending it to a good friend with a letter, helping the friend to remember who was who.
Write the letter, making this sort of comment about some of the people in the picture:

'. . . And the one on the far right with the long black hair and glasses was called Richard. I think he got married and is living . . .'

HIGHTOWN POLICE
WANTED
FOR
ARMED ROBBERY
IN HIGHTOWN
SATURDAY 9TH AUGUST 1988

HAVE YOU SEEN THIS MAN?
Height – 5ft 8ins: Age – 40–45:
Slight build: Light complexion:
Blond greasy shoulder-length
hair: Unshaven: High cheek
bones: Very small eyes.

YOUR ASSISTANCE IS
URGENTLY REQUESTED IN
TRACING THIS MAN

Any information to Hightown Police

UNIT 14

How can I help you?

A1 Multiple-choice items in Section A of the Reading Comprehension Paper sometimes test your knowledge of grammar. Look at this example, then do items 2–5.

> 1 In the office, routine jobs are often _____.
>   A neglecting B to neglect C neglected D neglect
>
> Choice **C** is the correct answer. Why?

2 Hold the racket _____ you can control it easily.
   A so that B because C in case D so as

3 I think you'll find that these ornaments need _____ regularly.
   A to polish B polishing C being polished D to have polished

4 _____ a computer can't help with this sort of problem.
   A Also B Even C Yet D Except

5 Take care _____ yourself.
   A not to hurt B not hurting C you didn't D don't hurt

A2 This extract is from an information booklet on teeth care. Read it, then compare, with a partner, what it says about the way you look after your own teeth.

The Good Brushing Guide

1 The inside surfaces of the teeth are easily neglected – so clean them first. Hold the toothbrush so that the filaments point at an angle. Do not scrub your teeth – use short vibratory back and forth movements.
2 Now clean the outside surfaces of all your teeth. Keep holding the brush head at an angle and use the short vibratory brushing action.
3 Finally clean the biting surfaces of all your teeth. Hold the brush filaments flat onto the teeth, using the short vibratory brushing action to remove food particles from the grooves and crevices. Take care not to brush too vigorously.

The Importance of Cleaning Between the Teeth

Each tooth has five separate surfaces that need cleaning to protect them against decay. Careful brushing removes plaque from the front, back and biting surfaces of the teeth. But even the finest conventional toothbrush cannot remove plaque from the sides. For this job, you need either dental floss, dental sticks, or an interdental toothbrush.

What is Dental Floss?

Dental Floss looks like a single thread, but in fact is made of over a hundred fine filaments designed to spread across the sides of your teeth for efficient plaque removal.

A3 Read the extract again and answer these multiple-choice questions:

1. The *Good Brushing Guide* stresses the importance of
   A regular brushing of one's teeth.
   B the correct action when brushing.
   C leaving the biting surface until last.
   D using the right sort of toothbrush.

2. The extract suggests that an interdental toothbrush
   A is really just like a conventional one.
   B should be used with dental floss.
   C can help to remove plaque.
   D is better than a conventional one.

3. What is one feature of Dental Floss?
   A It is the best way of cleaning the tops of teeth.
   B It is quite complex in its construction.
   C It only works with dental sticks.
   D It is only effective if one particular method is used.

4. What has using Dental Floss got in common with brushing?
   A The upper and lower teeth are treated in the same order.
   B One should always rinse food particles away.
   C The movement is always up and down.
   D One shouldn't be too vigorous in one's movements.

How to Use Dental Floss

A simple and effective method of flossing that many dentists recommend is as follows:

1. Cut off 60cms of floss and wind around your middle fingers.

2. Stretch the floss between right thumb and left forefinger. Keep about 3cms of floss between them. Starting with the right upper teeth, insert the floss carefully between the teeth, then clean each side of the teeth by pulling floss gently up and down. Clean right up to the gum margin, taking care not to damage the gums by too vigorous flossing.

3. For the left upper teeth, stretch floss over left thumb and right forefinger and repeat the procedure.

4. For all lower teeth, stretch floss between your two forefingers.

5. Use a fresh portion of floss for each space, unwinding floss from one finger, and taking up slack on the other.

6. After flossing, rinse the mouth to get rid of plaque which you have dislodged.

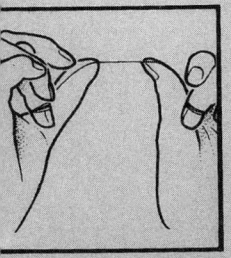
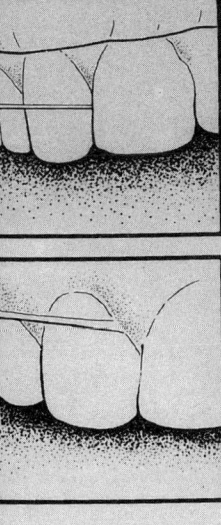

B One kind of 'speech' composition you might have to write is one in which you have to give advice, instructions or warning(s).

B1 First of all, look at these numbered sentences. What do you think each is referring to? Where do you think you would hear each of them? How would you describe each one? As a warning? Instructions? Advice? Or more than one of these?

1 If I were you, I'd wait until the top's just a little bit brown before taking it out of the oven.
2 The best way of doing it is to make a hole in the earth with your finger and just drop the seeds in.
3 Be careful you don't let the mixture become too hard; otherwise it'll be difficult to get smooth when it's actually on the wall.
4 Whatever you do, don't get it on your hands. It won't wash off and it can be quite painful.
5 Your wrist's still not flexible enough when you play an overhead shot. Try moving your hand up and down for a minute without the racket. And make sure you keep your arm still.
6 The last thing you want to do is to give yourself a nasty cut, so always pick it up by the handle, never the blade.

B2 In general terms, we can divide the language we use when giving instructions and advice into the following groups. Study the language, then do the exercise. (You can replace *do this/do that* phrases by appropriate verb phrases.)

Instructions	[Do this] first. Don't [do that] until you've [done this]. [This] must be [done] before you go on to the next step. Make sure you [do this] while [that is happening]. First, [do this]. Then [do that]. Next [do this]. Finally [do that].
Advice	If I were you, I'd [do that]. / You should [do this]. It might be an idea to [do this] before you [do that]. Or you could try [doing that] while you're [doing this].
Warning	Whatever you do, make sure you don't [do that]; otherwise [this] will/might [happen]. Be careful you don't [do that], or else [this] will [happen]. Take care not to [do that]; if you do, [this] will/could [happen]. Never [do this] without [doing that] first.

For each of the following tasks, use the prompts to give one instruction, one piece of advice and one warning. Look at this example:

To paint a room:
Make sure you stir the paint well first.
If I were you, I'd start at the top of the wall in case the paint drips.
Whatever you do, don't forget to wash the brushes when you've finished. Otherwise they'll go hard.

1 To prepare vegetables: wash / cut / not overcook – taste horrible
2 To plant flowers: dig / water / not plant when below zero – die
3 To push-start a car: take handbrake off – put car into second gear / get two strong people to help / not try to start engine until car is . . . – not start
4 To write a composition: make a plan and some notes / decide what is going to go in each paragraph / check – a lot of mistakes

B3 Study these structures, then write more sentences like them with the prompts given. In each case, decide which prompt should be used first.

Don't switch on *until* you have checked everything.
Only switch on *when/after* you have checked everything.

1 do the second part / do the first part
2 sign the letter / read it
3 turn off the gas / the water boil
4 the record – finish / turn off the record player
5 the first coat – dry / paint a second coat
6 start the composition / make a plan
7 read the question carefully / write an answer
8 buy the ring / she – agree to marry you

C In the First Certificate, you may be asked to write what you would say if you had to explain to someone how to do something e.g. how to cook a particular dish, use a piece of equipment or play a game. Here is a typical First Certificate composition:

> 'You are explaining a (card or dice) game to a friend. Write what you would say as you explain how to play.'

Think of a game. Then look at the notes below and see how they can help you as you write the explanation. The ideas in brackets are possible options, but you can of course use your own ideas.

First, you form teams of [. . . two? three? four?]. Then you place the [. . . pieces? cards? counters?] on the [. . . board? table? floor?]. When you've done that, one member of each team [. . . throws the dice? turns over the first card? calls out a number?]. You/They/Your opponent(s) have to [. . . move your/their counter? play another card? answer the question?]. If they [. . . can't go? haven't got a similar card? don't know the answer?], they [. . . lose a turn? have to stop? have to start again?]. This goes on until one team [. . . have played all their cards? reached the centre square? answered all the questions correctly?].

At any time during the game, a team can [. . . exchange their cards with those in the pile in the middle? consult a dictionary? challenge the other team(s)?]. The winning team is the one that . . . .

If I were you, I'd choose a partner (or partners) who [. . . has/have different interests from you? has/have played before? understand(s) the rules?]; otherwise you [. . . won't know what's going on? are bound to lose? might have problems?].

While you're actually playing, the best thing to do is to [. . . play safe? let your partner answer? keep your best cards until the end?]. Whatever you do, don't [. . . show your opponents what you've got? move your counter onto a red square? answer too quickly?].

Anyway, I'm sure you would enjoy it. It's the sort of game that . . ., and it's great fun.

UNIT 15

What's the solution?

A1 The article opposite appeared in *The Times* on 24th July 1986. Before you read the article itself, look at the headline, the brief introduction, the photo and the graph, and answer this question:

What is the article going to be about?

A2 Now answer (or ask and answer) these more specific questions:

1 Did the headline tell you clearly what the article would be about?
2 What did you learn from the 'introduction'? Did it state the problem clearly?
3 What was the effect of the photograph?
4 What did you learn from the graph? Did it tell you any more than you had already learned so far? Why?/Why not?

A3 Now, in pairs (helping each other), or on your own (and using a dictionary if necessary), read the article carefully and answer these questions:

What is the problem?/What are the problems?
Has anyone suggested a solution to the problem(s)? If so, what is it?/are they?

IMPORTANT: There will often be words and expressions in a text that you do not understand. Unless they are vital to understanding the text, try to learn to ignore them.

A4 Read paragraphs 1 and 2 again. Are these statements true or false? Why?

1 In 1984 about 3,000 young teenagers were killed or seriously injured on British roads.
2 Mr Frank West-Oram is the vice-chairman of the European Road Safety Year conference.
3 Children's deaths are hidden by the general rise in road casualties.
4 Despite what people think, British roads are safer for pedestrians now.

A5 Study this multiple-choice example and then do items 2–5 on page 64.

1 Why might more pedestrians be killed or injured than any other road users in the 1990s?
   A Because of the increase in traffic.
   B Because fewer drivers are being killed or injured.
   C Because of the attention of road safety engineers.
   D Because more people are driving everywhere.

Answer: The question refers to paragraph 3 (beginning 'The Department of Transport') and the first few lines of paragraph 4.

A: False. This might well be true – if the amount of traffic does increase, more pedestrians might be killed in the 1990s – but the text does not say so.
B: Correct. There has been 'a decline in casualties among motorists', so pedestrians might well be 'the largest single road-user casualty group in the 1990s'.
C: False. Peter Bottomley has suggested that road safety engineers should start to think more about people than vehicles.
D: False. The text says nothing about more people driving everywhere.

62

Putting safety first

Adult casualties may have fallen but more children than ever are being killed on Britain's roads

★ *sleeping policeman* a narrow raised part placed across a road to force traffic to move slowly

★★ *'Green Cross Code'* a set of rules for children to follow when learning how to cross a road

During the late 1950s about 1,500 young teenagers were killed or badly injured on the roads in Britain every year. By 1984 the toll had doubled. These figures and the masking of their relentless rise will be raised at a European Road Safety Year conference at Guildhall, City of London, today by Frank West-Oram, vice-chairman of the Pedestrians' Association.

"This killing of children is a national disaster but it is obscured by the decline in road casualties as a whole", he says. "Among reasons for that general decline are stronger cars, the wearing of seat belts and less walking. The result is that people think the roads are safer, although for pedestrians they are becoming more and more dangerous."

The Department of Transport is aware of these facts. David Smith, head of road safety, said earlier this year that the decline in casualties among motorists "seems likely to leave pedestrians the largest single road-user casualty group in the 1990s".

Peter Bottomley, Minister for Roads, has gone further than any of his predecessors in advising road safety engineers to switch their attention from vehicles to people. "A third of all journeys are made entirely on foot. Most other journeys involve walking to some degree. That must make pedestrians the most important class of road user. Too often planners seem to forget that", he said in April. But no successful action for reducing teenage casualties has yet been taken.

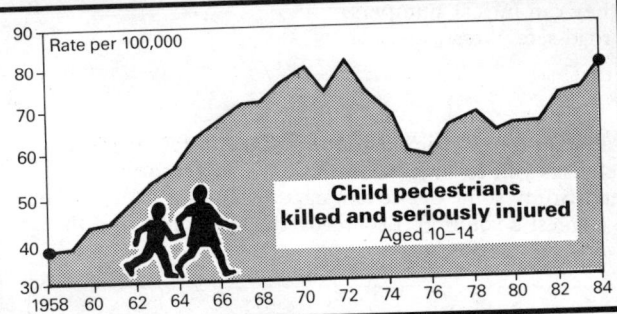

"The first priority is to do something about the speed at which drivers travel in towns", Mr West-Oram said. "We know from the work of Professor Ian Howarth at the University of Nottingham that casualties occur in residential areas because drivers ignore children and not the other way round. We need to narrow the roads and ★use sleeping policemen to slow down cars", he said.

"The Pedestrians' Association wants to see better policing and improved driver training as well. In Norway you get a driving licence only after passing two tests. You receive a provisional licence after the first but it is made permanent only after another test, a year later. Something similar should be introduced for new drivers in Britain."

Reducing casualties among the 10-14s presents special difficulties. Such children are beginning to explore on their own and tend to give up the "Green Cross Code" ritual.★★

They learn to cross the roads by copying adults. In time most successfully master the dangerous trick of choosing a gap in the traffic, aiming for the rear bumper of the car ahead of it, and marching into the road.

Before the year is over about 3,000 young boys and girls will fail this test. They will be killed or hurt. To some extent this is not surprising, since nowhere are children taught that the way most adults cross the roads is both difficult and stupid.

Terence Bendixson

2 What is the first thing that must be done to reduce pedestrian casualties?
   A More traffic-free zones must be created.
   B People should use public transport more, and not walk everywhere.
   C Drivers must be made to travel at slower speeds in towns.
   D Town planners must study more carefully the needs of drivers.

3 What's the reason for most accidents in towns, according to the experts?
   A The increase in traffic.
   B Children ignoring drivers.
   C Narrow streets.
   D Drivers not paying enough attention.

4 Why does Mr West-Oram refer to Norway?
   A He suggests they have a better driving test system than Britain.
   B Fewer people are killed on the roads there than in Britain.
   C Their police are more strict with drivers.
   D They have two tests – a written and a practical.

5 Which 'test' will 3,000 youngsters fail this year?
   A Their driving test.
   B A test to see if they can hit car bumpers.
   C A 'crossing the road safely' test.
   D A cycling test.

B1 A First Certificate 'argument' composition can take different forms. Here is the kind which asks you to suggest a solution (or alternative solutions) to a problem. Study some of the language we might use to ask or pose the question, to suggest a solution (or alternative solutions), and to give examples. Then do exercise **B2**.

Posing the question	So what is/might be the answer to this (terrible) problem? What, then, is the solution (to the problem)? (So) what can be done about it/the problem?
Suggesting a solution . . .	The most sensible solution to the problem is/would be for X to do Y. The first priority is to do something about . . . What⎫ The first thing⎭ we need to do is (to) [do] . . . What is needed is a . . . [This] should be [done]. / This is what should be done: . . .
or alternative solutions . . .	One answer may/might be for X to do Y . . . On the other hand, . . . might consider [doing] . . .
Giving an example	This solution has been most effective/very successful in [place]. This is one solution that has worked (very) successfully/with considerable success in [place], for example.

B2 Situation: You are at a meeting to discuss various problems at work. Here are some of the problems which are discussed and some suggested solutions which you agree with. Rewrite the solutions with the words given in brackets.

Problems
– The canteen is too crowded at lunchtime.

– The morning post is being delivered to departments very late.

– The temperature in the offices: some complain it's too hot, for some it's too cold.
– There have been too many accidents outside the factory.
– Staff have been complaining about feeling sick.

Solutions
1 We need to have a number of different lunchtime 'sittings'. (*Yes, what . . .*)
2 Someone from each department should fetch their post from the Post Room. (*I agree. The most sensible solution . . .*)
3 Each office should have its own thermostat so that they can regulate the heating. (*Yes, one answer . . .*)
4 The first thing we need to do is to impose a speed limit outside the factory. (*I agree. What . . .*)
5 The first thing we need to do is to find out what is making people feel ill. (*The first priority . . .*)

C Here is a typical First Certificate composition of this kind in which you have to suggest a solution (or alternative solutions) to a problem.

> 'In many countries of the world, large cities and even small villages in the countryside are becoming dirtier and dirtier. What do you think can be done about the problem?' (120–180 words)

Note: you are *not* asked to say whether you agree, *nor* what you think the causes of dirtier cities might be (if in fact it is true). Nevertheless, think about the possible causes, because you might want to refer to them in suggesting solutions.

Here are some notes you might make. Study them, discuss them and add any more points you can think of. Then write the composition.

Paragraph 1 (Stating the problem and posing the question)
– True – many cities, towns and villages – dirtier and dirtier
– Different kinds of dirt:
  caused by untidiness – litter thrown down;
  caused by laziness – people don't bother to clean streets, houses, etc.;
  caused by animals, cars, etc.;
  caused by industry – smoke, gases, dust.
– What's the solution? – or different solutions?

Paragraph 2 (Suggesting solutions – individual behaviour)
– Educate people to be tidier – and fines for litter;
– Encourage people to take more pride in surroundings;
– Suggest ways animals and cars could be less of a problem e.g. dog-free areas, lead-free petrol.

Paragraph 3 (Suggesting solutions – government action)
– Spend more public money on keeping cities, towns and villages clean;
– Help and encourage industry to reduce air pollution;
– Find different ways of disposing of waste from factories, etc.
Give examples of solutions used in certain countries.

Paragraph 4 (Conclusion: summing up)
– These – just some solutions to problem – but will take time and money.

UNIT 16

What can you do about it?

A1 Multiple-choice items in Section A of the Reading Comprehension Paper often test your knowledge of collocations – the way certain words always appear with others – a certain verb with a noun, an adjective with a noun, etc. For example, we say *get something* **wrong**, NOT '*get something false*', and **take** *a delight in*, NOT '*have* or *do a delight in*'. Study this example, then do items 2–5.

> 1 Most large stores would put 'good customer _____' high on a list of principles for running a good business.
> **A** friendship **B** relations **C** neighbours **D** acquaintances
>
> Choice **B** is the correct answer. Why?

2 There is _____ point in asking him for any help: he's far too selfish.
 A small **B** hardly **C** short **D** little

3 When complaining about anything officially, it's important to know your legal _____.
 A standards **B** duties **C** rights **D** powers

4 It's worth taking the _____ to write compositions as neatly as you can.
 A trouble **B** worry **C** carefulness **D** risk

5 If anything should go wrong with the machine, the company will _____ it right immediately.
 A have **B** do **C** put **D** turn

A2 Have you ever complained about goods or services? Tell the class or a partner about it: when, what you complained about, how (in person or in writing), and what happened.

A3 This extract is from a consumer magazine report 'Getting Action On Complaints'. Cover the 'CHAMPIONS' CHECKLIST' opposite and read the first part below.
What would *you* do in the different situations described in the text?

DON'T LET THEM GET AWAY WITH IT

You buy a pair of shoes and the first time you wear them the heel falls off. The builders *still* haven't been back to your house to put right the work they got wrong in the first place. Your neighbours regularly wait until you've got the week's washing on the line before burning their garden rubbish. And the council seems to have designated the road in front of your house as a permanent practice zone for apprentice hole-diggers.

What do you do: dither, miss your chance to complain firmly, and then kick yourself for letting them get away with it? If you wish you could do better when it comes to complaining and getting action, follow our Champions' Checklist and learn from other readers' successes and failures.

A4 Now read this 'CHAMPIONS' CHECKLIST' and answer the multiple-choice questions.

CHAMPIONS' CHECKLIST

Last May we asked for your help and many of you wrote in to tell us about your complaining tips and problems. Some of you would certainly qualify for the title Champion Complainer – though we don't know how much you'd like to be saddled with it! We've included the best of the tips in our checklist.

✓ **Ask yourself what you want** Before you start out in pursuit of a complaint, you should ask yourself what you want to achieve. It's straightforward enough if you want something putting right for yourself. But often, the best you'll get will be an apology, or the hope that things might improve for the next customer. Are you prepared to carry on?

✓ **Know your rights** But don't be too quick to quote them. Give shops, for example, a chance to sort things out as part of good 'customer relations'. And a little humour can lessen the sting.

✓ **Complain as soon as possible** The longer you delay, the weaker your legal rights may be, and the less sympathy you are likely to get from the firm at fault.

✓ **Complain to the right person** There's little point in tackling a British Rail ticket collector if you lose your money in a platform chocolate machine. Get the name and address of the right person – switchboards may help. Marking your letter for the personal attention of the named individual can be a good ruse. It's sometimes worth going straight to the top.

✓ **Go yourself** If you can manage it, it's worth turning up in person, at least for the first round. With a friendly manner, your problem may be solved there and then.

✓ **Follow up in writing** Type your letter (or at least write legibly), don't forget to date it and give your name and address. Try to anticipate excuses and demolish them.

✓ **Keep the paperwork** Keep copies of your letters to them, and their letters to you, receipts, dates of telephone calls, and notes of when things went wrong etc.

✓ **Stick at it** Don't give up when the going gets rough, unless it really does look as though the costs will exceed the gains.

✓ **Praise when it's due** There are some people who seem to take a delight in complaining about even the most trivial things. But they never think of praise. Yet taking the trouble to remark on good service can also improve standards.

1 What is the purpose of the 'Champions' Checklist'?
   A To suggest the kind of language to use when complaining.
   B To propose a number of alternatives to complaining.
   C To list a number of pieces of advice to do with complaining.
   D To help anyone writing a letter of complaint.

2 You should 'ask yourself what you want' because
   A you may have to accept just an apology.
   B complaining is always very difficult.
   C you might not have a right to complain.
   D a shop, for example, might be funny about things.

3 If you wish to make a complaint, the advice is this:
   A always write a letter to the person you are complaining about.
   B complain to the right person as quickly as possible.
   C sit and think about your legal rights first.
   D never complain immediately.

4 Why does the Checklist suggest you might try complaining in person (or face to face) first of all?
   A So that you won't need to keep copies of letters and so on.
   B Because you might just be offered weak excuses.
   C So that you don't spend money on postage and telephone calls.
   D Because you might be able to solve the problem on the spot.

UNIT 16

B One of the letter types that sometimes appears in the Composition Paper 2 is a letter of complaint or a letter asking what a company can do about something which is not working, etc. Often it is connected with explaining what has gone wrong (a fault or condition) and requesting action, or compensation.

Here is some of the language you will almost certainly want to use in a letter of this kind. Study it and write a few sentences that you might use in a letter complaining about a holiday that went wrong.

Expressing annoyance, surprise, etc.	I was rather/extremely annoyed to discover that . . . To my annoyance/surprise/amazement, [the first time I switched it on, . . .] (You can) imagine how annoyed I was when . . .
Explaining a fault	The problem is this: [the machine just won't start.]
Requesting action	I would be grateful/I would appreciate it if you could/would { give this matter your immediate attention. deal with this matter promptly/as soon as possible.

C1 Here is a typical First Certificate letter in which you are expected to complain about goods, explain a fault, and request action.

> 'You are spending some time in an English-speaking country. The new watch you bought only a fortnight ago in a town a few hundred miles away is not working properly. Write a letter to the shop expressing your annoyance, explaining the fault or problem, and asking what they can do about it.'

Decision time!
The situation is quite clear, but before you write, there are a number of things you must decide:

1 You might have to invent an address where you are staying in the English-speaking country – England? Australia? Canada? New Zealand? Ireland? On the other hand, if you *are* studying in an English-speaking country, use your real address.
2 You must invent a name and address for the shop.
3 You may need to invent and quote the date you bought the watch (a fortnight back from the day you sit the exam?), the number of the invoice and how much you paid. (And as with any real complaint letter, you must give any relevant information and reference numbers.)
4 You might want to describe, or give the name of, the shop assistant who served you. (And, by the way, was he or she polite? helpful? not very helpful?)
5 Decide what's wrong with the watch – and make sure you can describe the fault in English!
6 Decide what you want from the company: do you want an apology? do you want them to mend the watch? or replace it? do you want your money back? etc.

C2 Now write the letter about the watch, following the model and questions below. (For notes on the layout, beginnings and endings of formal English 'business' letters (and examples), refer back to Units 6 and 11, pages 29 and 49.)

```
                                    Flat 4, Old Town House,
                                    Harbour Walk,
    The Manager,                    Hightown
    'The Clock Shop',
    East Street,
    Middleton                       15th January 1988


    Dear Sir,

        I bought... [What in 'The Clock Shop'? When? For how much?]
    Since then... [What? Have you had nothing but trouble with it?
    Haven't you been able to use it? Hasn't it kept time at all? Has it been
    running fast/slow?]
        The first time I...[What? wore it? put it on? wound it up?]
    I was extremely annoyed to discover that... [What?]
    The problem is/seems to be this: [the watch...]
        I would like to know what you can do about it
    and would be grateful if you could/would... [What
    would you like the manager to do? Return your money? Offer to repair
    the watch free of cost? Or ...?]
        I enclose a copy of my receipt and would
    appreciate it if you could give this matter your
    immediate attention.
        [What do you look forward to doing?]


                    Yours faithfully,


                    [Sign your name here, and
                    print your name underneath]
```

C3 Now plan and write this letter:

> 'While as a student in an English-speaking country, you go on a long holiday weekend (by coach) organised by a local company. Almost everything you can think of goes wrong: it is in fact a disastrous weekend – and expensive! Write a letter to the company expressing your feelings and requesting some form of compensation.'

UNIT 17

What did you use to do?

A1 What's the most important annual festival for most people in your country? Is it New Year? Christmas? Midsummer's Day? Write down three adjectives, verbs, nouns and adverbs that come into your head when you think of how that festival was celebrated in the past. Then compare and discuss your list of words with one or two partners.

A2 Read this extract from an autobiography. These are the writer's recollections of his early Christmases. Does he have fond memories of them or not?

The turkey lunch, of course, dominated the day. The smell of very slightly burnt vegetable and meat hovered in the kitchen both before and for some hours after the meal.

We all put on our party hats at this stage, grandfather, I seem to recall, with a certain amount of controlled reluctance. Everyone expressed due approval after their first mouthful, except one year when something had gone disastrously wrong and that first mouthful was accompanied by a chorus of splutters.

After lunch the women would retire to the kitchen – or rather, the scullery as it was in those days – while the male members of the family sat and smoked, though probably not with much enjoyment, an annual fat cigar. It was, even then, a throwback to a bygone age of segregated partners following a meal.

We children used to be hurried off at this stage into the front room, where we played with the latest in plastic toys and tried on for the fourth time our new socks. We almost invariably behaved well. We thanked everybody profusely for the presents and declined another helping of Christmas pudding with great decorum. The only year I ever blotted my copybook was when I sulked for a good hour because my favourite carol was only played once during the all-round-the-piano singing of Christmas songs. I have a gnawing suspicion that my dear parents never forgot – or even forgave – that fit of bad temper.

At about four o'clock we would always gather around the card table and play for two hours. I suspect that nobody really enjoyed these games very much. Perhaps each generation thought it was doing the other two a favour. And yet the games were always keenly contested. An accusation of cheating would occasionally be heard.

At half past six there used to be more food: cold pork sandwiches, which I hated, sausage rolls and warm mince pies, which I adored. We used to sleep upstairs, in the so-called back room. It was a shapeless, characterless room with two small, extremely uncomfortable beds on one side and pictures of Victorian children on the walls. Grandmother would never change them. The brown wallpaper could not hide large patches of damp and there was an enormous wash-bowl on a chest of drawers in one corner. It was a most unattractive room and yet that night was the most magical, mystical night in the whole year. We were supposed to be asleep before nine, but we never were.

I was afraid every December that the magic was going to fade, but it never did.

A3 Now read the passage again and answer these multiple-choice questions.

1 What did they think of the turkey lunch?
   A It was generally disliked.
   B It was usually well received.
   C They always found it perfect.
   D It was not considered that important.

2 What was grandfather's attitude towards wearing a party hat?
   A He wore one willingly.
   B He protested a little.
   C He refused to wear one.
   D He couldn't wait to wear one.

3 Why did the men smoke cigars that particular afternoon?
   A The women were busy with other things.
   B The children weren't there.
   C They loved cigars.
   D It was Christmas.

4 The writer was upset one year. Why?
   A One of his books was spoilt.
   B He wanted a song to be played again.
   C He couldn't have any more Christmas pudding.
   D His parents wouldn't forgive him.

5 What do we learn about the card games they played?
   A They were taken seriously.
   B They were a highlight of the day.
   C They were spoilt by people cheating.
   D They were only played by some of the family.

6 The day that the writer describes was probably spent
   A in the writer's home.
   B downstairs in a Victorian hotel.
   C in the writer's grandparents' home.
   D upstairs in a hotel.

A4 Now try to work out the meaning of these words and expressions, many of which are probably new to you.

1 hovered
2 splutters
3 scullery
4 a bygone age
5 profusely
6 with great decorum
7 blotted my copybook
8 sulked
9 a gnawing suspicion
10 mystical

UNIT 17

B In the First Certificate Composition Paper you may be asked to describe a period in the past as well as narrate an experience that you had.

B1 Here is some of the language you might need to reminisce in English:

Single events	I *clearly remember going* into that room for the first time. I *shall never forget seeing* my best friend on television.
Regular events	We *used to sleep* in the garden on hot nights. Whenever I saw my aunt, she *would always give* me a penny. Grandmother *was in the habit of falling* asleep over meals. Grandfather *was always telling* us about his younger days.

Do you remember your first school? Think of one or two people there you liked and one or two that you didn't. Write sentences about them like this:

We had a student teacher there who would always put her arm round you if you fell down. And there was a little girl who was always giving everybody her sweets. I shall never forget seeing her cry one day because she didn't have one left for herself!

But there was one teacher who used to smack us quite hard if we didn't listen to what she was saying. And there was one horrible boy who was in the habit of pulling the girls' hair until they cried. I clearly remember running home in tears one day when he did it to me.

B2 With compositions such as 'Describe an accident you have witnessed or experienced' or 'The best/worst day in my life', past tenses (*did, was/were doing, had done, was going to do*, etc.) are extremely important. See how one small part of the first passage (end of paragraph 4, page 70) could be developed into a 'story'. Note particularly the forms of the verbs.

I was hoping and praying that they would ask me to sing my favourite carol to them. At about 7 o'clock, I thought they were going to have a break, so I went outside for a walk in the snow. Perhaps I should have asked what they were planning to do, but I didn't. If I had, the whole embarrassing episode wouldn't have taken place. While I was out, 'my' song was played and sung (and no doubt murdered!) by the rest of them. When I discovered what had happened, I sulked for an hour.

Here are two more examples of expanding a simple situation by using a range of past tenses. Put the verbs in brackets into a suitable form, and add a verb where there are empty brackets.

1 My mother (hope and pray) that the turkey (taste) all right. It (be) the first year that grandmother (allow) her to cook it. She (not know) that one of the children (come) into the kitchen while she (not look) and (pour) a packet of salt onto it. Perhaps she (should taste) it before she (serve) it, but she (not). If she ( ), the whole embarrassing episode (not take) place. When we (take) our first mouthful, there (be) a chorus of splutters. My mother (have) a red face for the rest of the day.

2 I (hope and pray) that he (be) at home. I (think) he (be) so pleased to see me. Perhaps I (should phone) him to let him know I (come), but I (not). If I ( ), the whole embarrassing episode (not take) place. When I (arrive), I (find) him dancing with another girl. As soon as I (see) what (happen), I (burst) into tears and (tell) him that I (never speak) to him again!

C1 Let's try to combine a lot of the language you have practised in this Unit in one typical First Certificate composition:

> 'Describe a day you will never forget.'

First you're going to set the scene and then describe a particular event (or events) from 'that day'. Use or adapt the 'starters' and prompts, and answer the questions to produce the composition, adding anything else you feel you want to.

Paragraph 1
I used to go to a school called . . .   [What was the name of the school?]
It was a . . . with about . . .   [What was it like? How big was it?/How many pupils were there in it?]

Every morning I would . . .   [What? – hurry my breakfast? rush about?]
and then my mother/father would . . .   [Did she/he walk you to school? take you in the car/van? walk you to the bus stop?]

She/He (or the bus?) used to leave me . . .   [Where? – 100 metres from the school? at the school gate? on the corner?]

and I had to walk . . . by myself.   [The rest of the way? the last 50 metres?]

Paragraph 2
There was one boy in the school, [name], who was in the habit of . . .   [Doing what?]
One day while I was . . .   [Doing what?]
he started running after me.
I didn't know what he . . .   [Wanted? was going to do?]
so I . . .   [What? – panicked? started screaming?]

Paragraph 3
I know I shouldn't have rushed . . ., but I did.   [Where?]
Just at that moment a/an . . .   [What?]
was coming along the road and the driver had to swerve . . .   [Why?]
He/She crashed into a/an . . .   [What?]
and his/her car/van (?) finished up . . .   [Where?]
I remember looking at it and thinking that the driver . . .   [What?]

Paragraph 4
When he saw what had happened, [name] . . .   [Did what? – ran away? disappeared?]
and I was left to . . .   [What?]
Fortunately the driver . . .   [How was he/she?]
but his/her . . . was . . .   [What condition was it in?]

C2 Now plan and write composition 17 on page 87.

UNIT 18

What's your own opinion?

A1 Before you start reading, briefly discuss these questions in small groups:

1 What difficulties do you think you would have had if you had had to change school quite often during your early education?
2 Even if parents have to move around the country, or even the world, are there good arguments for children to go, for example, into a boarding school? What do *you* think?

A2 Read this fictitious newspaper article, then answer the multiple-choice questions:

A certain amount of controversy has been caused by the publication of a new report by a team of educationalists from Coventry University, headed by Prof. B.J. Martin. The report claims to have statistical evidence that children who attend a number of different schools through their parents having to move around the country are more than normally prone to low academic achievement. There are also indications, says Professor Martin, of an unusually high rate of psychological disturbances among such children.

The professor, who has long suspected that the effect on children whose parents travel to different parts of the country in search of work has not been sufficiently researched, stresses that this is not simply an expression of prejudice. 'We're not dealing here with opinions,' he says. 'It's true, my personal feeling is that children should stay in one school. However, our findings are based on research and not on any personal attitudes that I or my colleagues may have on the subject.'

Capt. Thomas James, an Army lecturer for the past 20 years and himself a father of two, said: 'I've never heard such rubbish. As far as I'm concerned, absolutely no harm is done to the education of children who change schools regularly – as long as they keep to the same system, as in our Army schools. In my experience – and I've known quite a few of them – Army children are as well-adjusted as any others, if not more so. What the Professor doesn't appear to appreciate is the fact that in such situations children will adapt much better than adults.'

When this was put to Professor Martin, he said that at no time had his team suggested that *all* such children were backward or disturbed in some way, but simply that in their experience there was a clear tendency.

'Our findings indicate that while the extremely bright child can cope with regular upheaval without harming his or her general academic progress, the majority of children suffer from constantly having to enter a new learning environment.'

1 According to the first paragraph, Professor Martin's report suggests that
   A it may not be good for children to change schools too often.
   B parents should not move around the country.
   C statistics about education can be misleading.
   D psychological disturbances in children are becoming more common.

2 What do we learn about the professor's own personal opinion?
   A It is the opposite of what his report has shown.
   B It is in a way confirmed by his research.
   C It played a big part in his research.
   D It is based on his own experience as a child.

3 What can we conclude about Captain James' children?
   A They have been disturbed by changing schools.
   B They both go to ordinary State schools.
   C They have benefited from an Army school education.
   D They discuss their education regularly with their father.

4 In comparing children with adults, Captain James says that children are
   A normally better adjusted.
   B more adaptable.
   C less experienced.
   D able to cope just as easily.

5 According to Professor Martin, which children suffer most from changing schools regularly?
   A Exceptionally intelligent children.
   B Those of below-average intelligence.
   C Those from an Army background.
   D Normal children.

B One common type of First Certificate 'argument' composition is one in which you are asked to express your own opinion.

B1 There are many expressions you can use to preface an opinion. When writing a composition, these may be useful:

In my view, . . .	To my mind, . . .	My feeling is (that) . . .
In my opinion, . . .	As I see it, . . .	Personally, I feel (that) . . .

At what age do you think people should

1 start school? 5 start a family?
2 start work?   6 retire?
3 leave home?   7 be able to vote?
4 get married?

Express your own opinion using any of the 'starters' above.

But a composition may become monotonous if you simply express a string of opinions. Consider using a combination of these opening phrases as well:

Most people believe that . . ., but in my experience . . .
Some (people) would argue that . . ., but as far as I am concerned . . .
No one would deny that . . ., but it is still a fact that . . .
Many people seem to feel that . . ., but to my knowledge . . .

Study this example, then write similar sentences with the prompts below and using a variety of the phrases above.

> *Many people would argue that* military service is good for young men, *but in my own experience* it is a complete waste of time.

1 boarding schools – good for children / bad effect
2 doctors – just supply drugs / as important as ever
3 boxing – exciting sport / should be banned
4 television – should educate and inform / should entertain
5 zoos – wonderful places / degrading for animals

Now think of more examples yourself and write them down.

B2 A similarly balanced argument can be expressed using a combination of these phrases:

On the face of it, . . . but in reality . . .
At first sight, ... In fact, however, . . .
In theory, . . . but in practice, . . . (or However, in practice, . . .)
To a certain extent it's true that . . . . On the other hand, . . .
In some ways I agree with people who say that . . . . However, . . .
Up to a point it may be true that . . . , but overall I feel that . . .

Use some of the phrases above with the prompts below to make balanced points:

> *On the face of it*, English appears to be quite a simple language. *In fact, however*, it is a language of great complexity.

1 Space travel – a waste of money / . . .
2 Communism – the perfect system / . . .
3 America – the land of opportunity / . . .
4 The saying 'Life begins at forty' – true / . . .
5 Most pop music – could be written and played by chimpanzees / . . .
6 International sport – brings countries closer together / . . .

C1 Look at this headline and these extracts from three letters, then discuss the questions:

WHAT'S FOR BREAKFAST TODAY, MISS?

Sir,
  Breakfast in school (report November 25) is no novelty. In West Hartlepool, . . . by January, 1909, a daily average of 1,433 children breakfasted on 'a brown roll, currant bun and tea for each child, upon the five school days of the week'. Later, 'the question of continuing the currant bun was discussed. A suggestion to add a few more currants was agreed to' . . . Some of your readers may recall partaking of such fare.

Sir,
  I was delighted to read (report November 25) that Garth Hill Comprehensive School has now commenced serving breakfasts to pupils.

Sir,
  Whatever next? Television programmes in place of lessons. 'Project work' with the scantiest of supervision. And now breakfast in the classroom? . . . We seem to have forgotten that schools are places of learning. Of course children must be given breaks from work and obviously some form of lunch is necessary. But to start the day with a break! Where will it all end?

Would you be in favour of serving children breakfast at the start of the school day? Cover **C2** and make notes on the advantages and disadvantages as you see them.

C2 Compare your notes with these:

GOOD IDEA
- saves mothers work (especially working mothers)
- eating a social activity, brings children together
- ensures all children start day with some energy
- makes school feel like more than just a place for lessons

BAD IDEA
- the taxpayer has to pay (even those without children)
- bad effect on home life - breakfast is for the family
- institutional food often not good - no choice
- school is for learning, it's not a restaurant

C3 Now write this composition:

> 'Discuss the advantages and disadvantages of schoolchildren having breakfast at school. State the pros and cons, and give your own opinion.'

Paragraph 1
Introduction: Is this a new idea? Is it popular in your country?

Paragraph 2
State the arguments on the 'side' you don't really believe in yourself. Remember phrases like *Up to a point it may be true that* . . . and *Some would argue that* . . .

Paragraph 3
Concentrate on the other side of the argument, the one you believe to be stronger. Remember phrases like *In my experience,* . . . and *As far as I am concerned,* . . .

Paragraph 4
A balanced conclusion, but say which side of the argument you feel overall in sympathy with, for example: *To a certain extent it may be true that* . . ., *but on the whole I feel* . . .

C4 Now why not try composition 20 on page 87?

UNIT 19

How to tackle Paper 1 Reading Comprehension

General instructions for the whole Paper

Here are the instructions which are usually printed on the cover of Paper 1 Reading Comprehension. Read them, then answer the questions below:

> *Answer all questions. Indicate your choice of answer in every case* **on the separate answer sheet** *already given out, which should show your name and examination index number. Follow carefully the instructions about how to record your answers. Give* **one answer only** *to each question. Marks will not be deducted for wrong answers: your total score on this test will be the number of correct answers you give.*

1 How many questions must you answer?
2 Where do you mark your answers?
3 Will you receive the answer sheet before or after the question paper?
4 What else will be on the answer sheet? (Check that they are correct!)
5 Will they take away marks for wrong answers?
6 How will the examiner calculate your total score on this Paper?

A1 The Reading Comprehension Paper consists of two Sections and 1 hour is allowed for the Paper. **Section A** contains 25 multiple-choice items which you should try to complete in about 15 minutes. Complete this short sample test (only 8 items) in about 5 minutes before reading and discussing the page opposite.

SECTION A

In this section you must choose the word or phrase which best completes each sentence. **On your answer sheet** *indicate the letter A, B, C or D against the number of each item 1 to 8 for the word or phrase you choose.*

1 The man was so unpopular that one day someone _____ C _____ the tyres on his car.
   A pulled out   B let down   C blew out   D let off

2 _____ she was older than the rest, she still won the race.
   A In spite of   B Yet   C Although   D But

3 I didn't really want a watch, but the salesman _____ A _____ me to buy one.
   A persuaded   B talked   C suggested   D demanded

4 They had a beautiful _____ D _____ of the distant mountains from their window.
   A scenery   B oversight   C look   D view

5 He would never have met her if he _____ C _____ into the little sweet shop.
   A hadn't gone   B didn't go   C wouldn't have gone   D wouldn't go

6 The last time I saw him he was _____ shaven, but he's got a beard now.
   A clean   B well   C smooth   D good

7 After the storm, they had to _____ their roof repaired.
   A do   B have   C let   D make

8 _____ A _____ a certain extent I think you're right, but I can't agree with you completely.
   A In   B At   C On   D To

78

A2 Answers and Explanations

1B This is a test of phrasal verbs. You could *pull off* a tyre (if you were strong enough!), but not *pull one out*. You can *let down a tyre* (= let the air out of). *A tyre can blow out*, but *you can't blow out a tyre*, although you can *blow one up* (= put air into one). You can't *let off a tyre*, although you can *let out air* if the pressure is too high.

2C This is a grammatical item. For A to be correct, it would have to read '*In spite of the fact that she was older . . .*'. B and D would only be correct if the sentence read '*She was older than the rest, yet/but she still won . . .*'.

3A The clue is in the first part of the sentence ('I didn't really want a watch . . .'). B would only be correct if the sentence read '*talked me into buying one*' (= persuaded me to buy one). And C or D? Well, both would be wrong grammatically. You can't *suggest* or *demand someone to do something*.

4D This is really a question of collocation. You can *have a view of the mountains*, but you can't '*have a scenery*', '*an oversight*' or '*a look*'. (You *could have a look* **at** *the scenery*, of course, but this is not what is wanted here!)

5A This is a pure grammatical item. Choices B, C and D simply do not fit the sense or structure of the sentence.

6A There is a clue at the end of the sentence ('he's got a beard now'), but the answer relies mainly on collocation. We describe a man who shaves regularly as *clean shaven*: we cannot say '*well shaven*', '*smooth shaven*' or '*good shaven*', although we can say that a man has 'a smooth chin'.

7B This is another pure grammatical item. The structure is '*have something done*' or '*get something done*', and since 'get' is not given as an option, 'B have' must be correct.

8D This is a test of prepositional phrases used particularly in expressing opinions. The correct phrase is '*to a certain extent*'. Phrases with the other prepositions are '*in my opinion / in theory / in some ways*', '*at first sight*' and '*on the face of it*' (see Unit 18, page 76).

A3 Exam Advice: Golden Rules for Reading Comprehension Paper, Section A

1 Watch your *timing*. Don't spend more than 15 minutes on the 25 questions in this Section.

2 Read the *instructions* very carefully. You have read them often in practice, but you should always read them in the exam to make sure you have to do exactly the same.

3 Make sure you mark *the right letter* (A, B, C or D) on your answer sheet.

4 *Don't get stuck on one question:* you haven't got time! If you can't do one, leave it and come back to it at the end.

5 Make sure you write your answer against *the right question number* on the answer sheet.

6 *Don't leave any* questions *unanswered*!

7 *Read the whole sentence* before answering.

8 Think carefully about *the meaning of the whole sentence*.

9 Look for *grammatical and collocational clues* to the answer.

10 Well before the exam, *read as much and as widely in English* as you can.

UNIT 19

B1 Section B of the Reading Comprehension Paper contains 15 multiple-choice items which test your understanding of (usually) three passages. You should try to complete this section in about 45 minutes.

Complete this short sample test section in about 14 minutes before reading and discussing the answers and explanations opposite.

SECTION B

In this section you will find after the passage a number of questions or unfinished statements about it, each with four suggested answers or ways of finishing. You must choose the one which you think fits best. **On your answer sheet** *indicate the letter A, B, C or D against the number of each item 9–12 for the answer you choose. Give one answer only to each question. Read the passage right through before choosing your answers.*

It's interesting, the effect that the arrival of snow has on people in different countries. There are those countries for whom the arrival of the first snow showers is an expected annual event. There are those countries for whom the arrival of snow at any time of the year would be almost unheard of, and would be regarded as a major climatic catastrophe, or even a miracle.

But there are countries between these two 'extremes' that normally expect snow some time over the winter months, but never receive it regularly or in the same quantities every year. For them (and Britain is a prime example of such a country) the arrival of snow quite simply creates havoc. Within hours of the first snowfalls, however light, roads (including motorways) are blocked, train services are disrupted and bus services to suburbs and country districts are withdrawn. Normal communications quickly begin to suffer as well: telephone calls become difficult and the post immediately takes twice as long as usual. And almost within hours there are also certain shortages – bread, vegetables and other essentials – not because all these things can no longer be produced or even delivered, although deliveries are disrupted, but mainly because people panic and go out and stock up with food and so on – 'just in case'.

But why does snow have this effect? After all, the Swiss, the Austrians and the Canadians don't have such problems. The answer is quite simply a lack of planning and preparation – and we can't blame the weather forecasters for that. We have to remember, however, that equipment needed for dealing with snow and ice costs money. To keep the roads clear, for example, requires snowploughs and vehicles to spread grit or salt. The argument against investing in snowploughs in a country like Britain is that they are only used for a few days in any one year, and that money could more usefully be put into other things such as the hospital system, social services, helping the elderly, and so on.

9 According to the writer, Britain is a country
   A which expects snow every year.
   B that is always prepared for snow.
   C for which snow is a miracle.
   D which has extremes of weather.

10 What does the arrival of snow in Britain affect *most*?
   A Suburban life.
   B Food supplies in shops.
   C Social services and hospitals.
   D Travel and communications.

11 Why are there often shortages of food, for example?
   A Farmers cannot produce any more.
   B People buy as much as they can.
   C Bakeries have to close down.
   D People eat more vegetables in winter.

12 There are a number of reasons why the British are reluctant to invest in snowploughs. What is the first one given in the text?
   A Grit on roads is more effective.
   B Snowploughs are not used enough.
   C The hospital system is more important.
   D Old people need the money more.

UNIT 19

B2 Answers and Explanations

9A This is a question about the first paragraph and the first three lines of paragraph 2. Britain is quoted as an example of a country 'that normally expects snow some time over the winter months', so A is correct. Britain is obviously *not* prepared for snow, since it 'creates havoc', so B is wrong. C is wrong because snow is not 'a miracle' in Britain. And D is wrong because the text does not say that the country has 'extremes of weather': the 'extremes' mentioned are countries that do and do not have snow.

10D The important word in the question is the word *most*, and the question refers to the middle of paragraph 2 from the words 'Within hours . . .'. The references to 'roads', 'train services', 'bus services', 'telephone calls' and 'the post' all point to D as the correct answer. The other choices (A 'Surburban life', B 'Food supplies in shops' and C 'Social services and hospitals') are all referred to at some point, but are wrong as answers because they are not affected *most*.

11B This question refers to the last few lines of paragraph 2. A is wrong: the text does *not* say farmers can't produce any more. B is correct: the text says that 'people panic and go out and stock up with food' (= buy as much as they can). The text mentions a shortage of bread, but nothing about bakeries closing, nor does it say anything about people eating more vegetables, so C and D are also wrong.

12B You have to read the last paragraph for this question, and the last half in particular. As the question says, there are a number of reasons why the British are reluctant to invest in snowploughs. The first reason given is that 'they are only used for a few days in any one year'.

Exam Advice: Golden Rules for Reading Comprehension Paper, Section B

1 Watch your *timing* again, just as in Section A. Remember, you have to answer 15 multiple-choice questions on three texts in about 45 minutes. Do not spend most of your time on the first passage, then have to rush the others. Divide your time and be strict with yourself. Try to give yourself about 14 minutes for each passage.

2 Remember the same pieces of advice 1–6 as for Section A.

3 Read the multiple-choice questions, then the passage, and then the questions again *before* answering them.

4 Find the right part or parts of the text when doing each question. The answer may be in a few lines, or you may have to look at different parts of a text.

5 Read all four possible answers for each question *in detail* and don't choose the first you read which just *sounds* right or *looks* right. It may be, but it may not be! Check against the other possible answers and the text.

6 Don't automatically expect the next answer to come in the lines of the text following the last answer. It usually will, but not always.

7 Don't think that because a particular word appears in the text *and* in an answer (as in 9D above, for example) that that answer is therefore correct. Read the text and the choice carefully to see how that word is used or qualified.

8 Watch out for the meaning of punctuation and conjunctions, and notice little words like *it, that, those, he, she, too, so,* etc. and work out what they refer to. These words are often very important to the sense of a sentence.

UNIT 20

How to tackle Paper 2 Composition

Exam guidance for the whole Paper

This is an example of the sort of Composition Paper you can expect in the First Certificate exam. Read it carefully, then answer the questions below:

PAPER 2: COMPOSITION

Time: 1 hour 30 minutes

Write **two only** *of the following composition exercises. Your answers must follow exactly the instructions given, and must be of between 120 and 180 words each.*

1 You have just received a letter from an English-speaking friend inviting you to join him or her on a fortnight's holiday in Malta next summer. Write back accepting and asking for further information, *or* expressing regret and giving reasons why you won't be able to go.

2 Write an account of a journey that you will always remember.

3 Imagine you were given the chance to stand up at the United Nations and tell the world's leaders and politicians (in English) about the things that you really feel need to be done in the world today. Write what you would say.

4 'Why should boxing be banned? It's an exciting sport. And anyway, boxers aren't forced into taking part. They all know what they're doing.' What do you think about boxing and similar sports?

5 *(This will be a choice of questions on the prescribed texts.)*

---

1 How many compositions must you write?
2 How long is the exam?
3 How much time would you spend on each of the following:
   a reading the whole Paper and choosing?
   b writing the plan for your first composition?
   c writing your first composition?
   d checking your first composition?
   e writing the plan for the second composition? etc.
4 Would you have time to write a rough and a fair copy of each?
5 Which composition titles would you choose? Those that
   a interest you most?
   b seem easiest to write? or
   c a combination of **a** and **b**? Why?

Exam Advice: Golden Rules for the Composition Paper

1 Read the whole paper very carefully before choosing titles.

2 When choosing titles, think carefully about the language you will need.

3 Read the *instructions* very carefully and keep to them.

4 Make sure your compositions are 100% relevant to the titles.

5 Make sure you write compositions of the right length.

6 *Don't spend all your time on the first composition.* You must share your time equally between the two that you write.

7 For each composition, think what you want to write and make a plan.

8 Give yourself as much time as you can to check your work.

A brief revision of composition writing

Do all the following exercises to plan and write each of the compositions from the sample Paper opposite. You can work on your own or with a partner. We can't cover *all* the points again here, so refer to earlier Units as much as you need to.

An important reminder

When writing a composition, it is very easy to make mistakes – mistakes of all different kinds which you would not usually make. So *always give yourself time to check what you have written!* We suggest you allow 10–15 mins. for planning, 25–30 mins. for writing (a total of 40 mins. for planning and writing) and 5 mins. for checking. When you have written each composition, read and check it for: grammar, the correct vocabulary, . . . And what else should you check?

1 The Letter

> You have just received a letter from an English-speaking friend inviting you to join him or her on a fortnight's holiday in Malta next summer. Write back accepting and asking for further information, *or* expressing regret and giving reasons why you won't be able to go.

As you answer or discuss these questions, look again at the notes, exercises and letters in Units 1, 6, 11 and 16 of this book.

1 What kind of letter do you have to write – a personal letter or a 'business' letter? So what kind of language will you use – reasonably formal or informal?
2 Which of the following will you put at the top of the letter: your own name? your own address? your friend's name? your friend's address? the date?
3 Will you start the letter with 'Dear Sir or Madam, . . .'? And how will you end it? What form will you use: something like 'Yours faithfully, . . .'?
4 **Decision time:** Are you going to accept or refuse the invitation? If you are going to refuse, think of a good reason. (Remember that the friend might well have suggested dates for the holiday, so you will have to refer to them.)
5 This will probably be a simple letter of three paragraphs. What will you write in each?

2 The Narrative Composition

> Write an account of a journey that you will always remember.

As you answer or discuss these questions, look again at the notes, exercises and examples in Units 2, 7, 12 and 17 of this book.

1 Can you think of a journey that you will always remember? If so, make brief notes: when was it? how old were you at the time? was it a train journey, a journey by road, a sea voyage, an aeroplane flight? who was with you? how did you feel? what happened? why was it so memorable? etc. If you *can't* think of a journey, imagine one and make up answers to the questions above.

2 Try to tell the story in three stages: Paragraph 1 – Before the journey; then Paragraph(s) 2 (and 3?) – What?; and Paragraph 3 (or 4) – What?
3 You will be using past tenses e.g. *went* and *was eating*. What other tenses?
4 And you will be using joining words such as *when*, *as soon as* and *after*. Make a list of other joining words and phrases you may want to use.

3 The Description

A Composition Paper will rarely contain a narrative *and* a descriptive composition; generally you will have to write one or the other. The Paper on page 82, however, might have contained this composition:

> Describe, as if in your autobiography, the first family home (apartment or house) that you remember as a child.

As you answer or discuss these questions, look again at the notes, exercises and descriptions in Units 3, 8 and 13 of this book.

1 Think of your first family home and think how you will describe it. Jot down some rough ideas under paragraph headings.
   - Paragraph 1: Introduction: Where (town/village/street) was the house/apartment? How far was it from school/your father's work/the centre? Can you describe it in general terms? Can you describe the outside?
   - Paragraph(s) 2 (and 3): the inside of the apartment/house – number of rooms, some details of each, etc.
   - Paragraph 3 (or 4): Conclusion: What was it like when you left? Or, if you still live there, what is it like now? etc.
2 Picture the apartment or the house in your mind's eye and add, to the paragraph notes, words and phrases you want or need to use e.g. *veranda, large flower garden, small cold bathroom, stone floors, wall-to-wall carpeting*, etc.
3 What words or phrases can you think of to join ideas, such as *and*, *Although . . ., As well as . . .* and *Apart from . . .*? Make a list.

4 The Speech

> Imagine you were given the chance to stand up at the United Nations and tell the world's leaders and politicians (in English) about the things that you really feel need to be done in the world today. Write what you would say.

As you answer or discuss these questions, look again at the notes, exercises and 'speeches' in Units 4, 9 and 14 of this book.

1 What kind of 'speech' are you being asked to write – a formal, or an informal one? So how might you start? How would you address the audience?
2 What things *do* you think need to be done in the world today? Do we need to spend more on education in developing countries? Should we ban all nuclear arms? And what about the problems of crime, unemployment, human rights, and so on? Make a list of points you want to make. Then order them in the way you think they will have most effect – for example, the most important point first or last?

3 What about some of the language you will need?
 – What 'conditional' sentences might you want to use e.g. *If I had the power, I would . . .?*
 – And what about phrases to order your points e.g. *Firstly/First of all, . . ., Next/And then/Secondly, . . .* etc. Make a list of other phrases like this.
 – And what about expressing opinions? Starting with *In my opinion, . . .* make a list of phrases you might want to use.
4 How will you finish your 'speech'? Think carefully, and write two or three alternative closing sentences.

5 The Argument Composition

> 'Why should boxing be banned? It's an exciting sport. And anyway, boxers aren't forced into taking part. They all know what they're doing.' What do you think about boxing and similar sports?

As you answer or discuss these questions, look again at the notes, exercises and examples in Units 5, 10, 15 and 18 of this book.

1 Which of the following are you being asked to do: a) write in favour of boxing as a sport? b) write against boxing as a sport? c) write the arguments for *and* against boxing? or d) express your own opinion about boxing and other sports like it?
2 In order to express your own opinion, you will need to mention some of the pros and cons of the argument. On your own, or in discussion, make two lists of brief notes – one list in favour of boxing, the other against. (And by the way, what other sports are 'similar' to boxing for the sake of this argument?)
3 This will probably be a three-paragraph composition. What should go in each? (In other words, draft a brief plan of what you want to write.)
4 Do you remember the kinds of sentences that you can use when putting forward two sides of an argument: '*At first sight . . . . In actual fact, however, . . .*'? What other sentence patterns can you write down that you might be able to use?
5 Make notes for the composition under paragraph headings. If Paragraph 1 is an introduction of the theme, and Paragraph 3 (or 4) is a balanced conclusion with your own opinion, what will Paragraph(s) 2 (and 3) contain?

Twenty more composition topics

	Composition Type	Composition Exercise
UNIT 1	LETTER	You have just moved into a new flatlet, apartment or house, and would like a good friend to come and see it and spend a weekend with you. Write the letter, adding directions on how to get there.
UNIT 2	NARRATIVE	Describe one day in your life that you will never forget, either because it was so marvellous or because it was so awful.
UNIT 3	DESCRIPTION	Describe your ideal home.
UNIT 4	'SPEECH'	Two English-speaking friends have come to spend some time with you and you have taken them to school/college with you for a day. Write what you say as you show them around.
UNIT 5	ARGUMENT	Outline the advantages of *not* having a television in your home.
UNIT 6	LETTER	An English-speaking friend wrote to you a few weeks ago to ask your advice about whether he or she should leave school and get a job, or stay at school for another two years and go to college. Write apologising for not replying immediately, and telling him or her what you think.
UNIT 7	NARRATIVE	This is the last sentence of a story: 'That was the last time she ever spoke to him.' Write the story that led up to it.
UNIT 8	DESCRIPTION	You have recently started at a new school or college or started a new job. Describe, as if in a letter to an English-speaking friend, your new school, college or place of work.
UNIT 9	'SPEECH'	A sports club of which you are a member has been invited to another club to a one-day meeting. After the events have taken place, the two teams sit down to a meal together, and you have been asked to give a vote of thanks to your host team. Write what you would say.
UNIT 10	ARGUMENT	In the future, we shall probably have 'videophones'. (A videophone is a telephone which will allow speakers to see each other.) Would you have one? What advantages *and* disadvantages can you foresee?

	Composition Type	Composition Exercise
UNIT 11	LETTER	You are considering going to an American university to continue your studies. Write a letter to your nearest American Embassy requesting information regarding entrance requirements, specialist courses, methods of payment, etc.
UNIT 12	NARRATIVE	Write an account of a day or a weekend that changed your life.
UNIT 13	DESCRIPTION	As part of a 'witness observation test', you were shown a reconstruction of a bank robbery on television. Write a description of the three 'bank robbers' (two men and a woman) as if for the police.
UNIT 14	'SPEECH'	Your own native language most probably has sounds in it which are difficult for a foreign learner to produce. Write what you would say to such a person while you are helping him or her to make the sounds correctly.
UNIT 15	ARGUMENT	Sometimes three generations with very different attitudes and lifestyles live together in one family home. What are some possible problems, and what can be done to keep them to a minimum?
UNIT 16	LETTER	While on holiday in a town in an English-speaking country, you went to the local Information Centre to find out what to see, where to go, etc. Because of the lack of brochures and the negative attitude of the assistant, however, you came away with nothing. Write a strong but polite letter to the Tourist Services Manager stating your complaints and suggesting ways they might improve their service to holidaymakers and other visitors.
UNIT 17	NARRATIVE	Write an article for a magazine in which you describe your memories of being seven years old.
UNIT 18	DESCRIPTION	Describe any exciting sporting event you have taken part in or attended as a spectator.
UNIT 19	'SPEECH'	You are renting your apartment for a week to an English-speaking family you know. Write what you would say (pointing out, for example, how to use various pieces of equipment) as you show them round the kitchen and living-room.
UNIT 20	ARGUMENT	It has been said in some countries in recent years that parents expect too much of schools and that they (the parents) should contribute more to their children's education. What do *you* think?

Key to Exercises

This Key contains Unit-by-Unit answers to all exercises such as open comprehension questions, True/False statements, multiple-choice questions, sentence transformation, grammar practice, etc. It does not contain Phase C model compositions.

KEY: UNITS 1–3

UNIT 1 What about coming to see us?

A2 1 c; 2 a; 3 b; 4 d

A4 1 True; 2 True; 3 True; 4 True; 5 False; 6 False; 7 True; 8 False

B2 Possible completions:
1 . . . if you'd like to come to the theatre with us?
2 . . . for the invitation/ . . . for inviting me.
3 . . . love to come/ . . . be delighted to come.
4 . . . you like to come as well?
5 . . . very much for the invitation/ . . . for inviting me;
6 . . . I won't/shan't be able to come/go with you.

C3
1 'The Firs',
54, Larkshill Road,
Little Village,
Northington,
Surrey
21st March, 1987

2 Flat 6,
178, Bristol Road,
Southtown,
Yorkshire YY3 5AB

19 October, 1986

3 163, Westwood Avenue,
East Moors,
Ringwood,
Hampshire 12T B34
July 3, 1987

4 c/o Mr & Mrs James,
57, Long Drive,
Exbourne,
Kent,
England
23rd May, 1987

UNIT 2 What happened?

A1 2 C; 3 B; 4 D; 5 C

A3
1 A wristwatch; to have it repaired.
2 Twenty-six years ago.
3 Fourteen years old.
4 Eight years.
5 Nothing./Not a penny.

A4
1 It was a woman. She mentions her maiden name, her family name before she got married.
2 He had probably inherited it from his father; he was the son of the previous owner and his father had put the ticket on the watch.
3 Forty years old.

B1
1 I had plenty of time, so I didn't hurry./I didn't hurry because I had plenty of time.
2 She was very worried, so she asked her friend for some advice./She asked her friend for some advice because she was very worried.
3 The man was found guilty of stealing, so he went to prison./The man went to prison because he was found guilty of stealing.
4 I was lost, so I asked a passer-by the way to the Town Hall./I asked a passer-by the way to the Town Hall because I was lost.
5 I thought I was going to be late for my appointment, so I called a taxi./I called a taxi because I thought I was going to be late for my appointment.

B2
1 I checked the contents before I locked my suitcase./I locked my suitcase when/after I had checked the contents.
2 The journalist heard the judge's verdict before he rang his newspaper./The journalist rang his newspaper when/after he had heard the judge's verdict.
3 They watched the film before they began their discussion./They began their discussion when/after they had watched the film.
4 She went to see the doctor before she phoned her office./She phoned her office when/after she had been to see the doctor.
5 I read all about the computer before I went and bought one./I went and bought the computer when/after I had read all about it.

UNIT 3 What's it like?

A1 They are taken from:
1 stage directions for a play;
2 a leaflet about a castle or historic house;
3 a personal letter or postcard;
4 a newspaper report;
5 a novel or autobiography.

A2 a 4; b 3; c 2; d 1

A3
1 Derby Avenue (no town/city mentioned);
2 '. . . attempts were being made today';
3 'The owners . . . are believed to be on a touring holiday.'
4 'splendid 18th-century house', 'valuable antique furniture' and '£45,000 worth of damage'.
5 'The fire was thought to have been started by a gas explosion.'
6 '18th-century house';
7 It was a house, and 'first-floor rooms' are mentioned.
8 Neighbours were worried and there were eye-witnesses.

A4 1 False; 2 False; 3 False; 4 True; 5 True; 6 True

B1 1 twisted; 2 worn; 3 torn; 4 stained; 5 faded; 6 damp; 7 peeled; 8 cracked; 9 rusty; 10 dust; 11 grease

B2
1 All the rubbish had been cleared away and nice evergreen bushes had been planted.
2 The centre light has been replaced by wall lights and an old-fashioned fireplace has been put in.
3 All the furniture had been moved around and a new photocopier, computer and coffee-machine (had been) installed.
4 Two rooms have been converted into one and the small bedroom has been turned into a shower room.

And with *have something done*:
1 They had had all the rubbish cleared away and had had nice evergreen bushes planted.
2 We have had the centre light replaced by wall lights and (have) had an old-fashioned fireplace put in.
3 They had had all the furniture moved around and (had had) a new photocopier, computer and coffee-machine installed.
4 They have had two rooms converted into one and (have had) the small bedroom turned into a shower room.

KEY: UNITS 4–7

B3 1 The windows are very dirty. They need cleaning.
2 The wooden floors look very dull. They need polishing.
3 The curtains are filthy. They need washing.
4 The door hinges are rusty. They need oiling.
5 The woodwork is nearly bare. It needs painting.
6 Some floorboards are loose. They need nailing down.
7 The carpets are filthy. They need shampooing.

UNIT 4 What's happening?

A1 2 B; 3 A; 4 B; 5 B

A2 (The writer is sitting) in a spaceship/on the flight deck of a spaceship.

A3 1 False; 2 False; 3 True; 4 True; 5 True; 6 True; 7 True; 8 False; 9 False; 10 True

A4 These are the words connected with sound or noise: high-pitched; deafening; ringing; whirring; clicking

A5 2 A; 3 A; 4 A; 5 B

UNIT 5 Are you for or against?

A1 The recent editorial was about the pros and cons of students doing part-time work. It almost certainly suggested that students should not have a part-time job.

A2 2 B; 3 B; 4 A; 5 B; 6 B

A3 1 Paragraphs 2, 3 and 4.
2 Possible summaries:
Paragraph 2: Working can give students useful experience of the real world.
Paragraph 3: The money students earn can help their families financially.
Paragraph 4: With a part-time job students can help society as well as themselves.
3 Points:
– jobs in which students learn to get on with a lot of different people.
– families which need extra income.
– work which students can do which is useful to the community.
– things that Mrs Williams' father thought teenagers should be interested in.
– things that Mrs Williams hopes her daughter won't waste her time on.
4 She talks more about herself and her own family here than the objective pros and cons of the argument.

B1 Possible answer:
The first point I would like to make in favour of paying everybody the same wages or salary *is that* most people work about the same number of hours. *Another strong argument for* paying everyone the same *is that* all jobs are important. *And another reason for* equal salaries is that unskilled work, often paid less at present, is not as much fun or not as interesting as skilled work, so why should we pay less for that? *And last but not least we should remember that* most religions say that all people should be treated as equals.

UNIT 6 What's your excuse?

A1 The extract is probably from a thriller or detective story.

A2 1 Because he was still thinking about the meeting.
2 Because they had not received an apology from Ray Wallace for his absence.
3 The name James Read.
4 He went into the lounge and sat at his desk.
5 Not attending the meeting.
6 He had received another letter or note from the kidnapper.
7 Because he suspected one of the committee members.
8 Because he said he had better warn the others that Ray suspected something.

A3 1 That was the year the story took place.
2 That was the time Ray was told to go to the churchyard.
3 That was how much Ray was told to take.
4 That was the telephone number James dialled.

A4 2 (When did James open and read the letter?) C;
3 (How had the kidnapper contacted Ray Wallace?) B;
4 (Why did Ray Wallace write his letter on 'Vicarage' notepaper?) C

B2 1 My advice to you is not to tell anyone about it.
2 Please accept my apologies for not telephoning you to discuss the problem.
3 I really must apologise for not returning your book before.
4 You would be (well) advised to forget the whole thing.
5 The best thing you can do is to think the matter over again.
6 Sorry I left/Sorry for leaving you to arrange everything.
7 I think you should talk to a solicitor.
8 I'm sorry I ('ve) caused/I'm sorry for causing you so much trouble.

UNIT 7 How did it end?

A2 It's probably going to be about an accident involving two vehicles, one of which sinks in water with a girl inside.

A3 1 a 31; b More than 20 minutes; c 15 yards; d 40 minutes; e the A26
2 a Kevin; b Susan; c Tarring Neville; d Bishopstone; e a Ford Escort; f Coldharbour Road, Upper Dicker, Sussex

A4 1 True; 2 False; 3 False; 4 True

B1 1 The guard opened the door, looked out, shone his torch right at me, shouted, took out his revolver, and fired.
2 The bird hovered for a few moments, caught sight of a movement below, plunged into the long grass, and flew out carrying a mouse in its beak.
3 I ran to my car, got in, closed the door, started the engine, put it into first gear, and drove off as fast as I could.

KEY: UNITS 8–11

B2 1 Being old and weak, he couldn't do much to help.
2 Realising that he had to keep her conscious, Mr Holland kept talking to her.
3 Thinking that perhaps the driver of the second car could help, he called to him.
4 Having been given the wrong location, they spent a long time looking for the scene of the accident.
5 Not wanting any publicity, they drove off without giving their names.

UNIT 8 Can you describe the place?

A1 2 B; 3 A; 4 C; 5 D

A2 Text A is from a factual brochure about Jersey. Text B is taken from a personal letter. Text C is from a newspaper article.

A3 1 False; 2 True; 3 False; 4 False; 5 True; 6 False; 7 False; 8 False

B1 1 –; 2 the; 3 –; 4 the; 5 –; 6 the; 7 –; 8 the; 9 –; 10 –; 11 –; 12 –; 13 –; 14 –; 15 the

UNIT 9 What can I say?

A3 1 accolade; 2 trance; 3 glimpse; 4 humble; 5 platitudes; 6 joint; 7 reluctance; 8 trace

A4 1 C; 2 B; 3 C; 4 B; 5 D; 6 B

B2 Possible answers:
1 I'd like to thank you for an absolutely marvellous evening. I *did* enjoy it.
2 This must be the most wonderful day in my life.
3 He has been a truly wonderful friend to me for as long as I can remember.
4 She must be one of the most superb actresses alive.
5 I'd like to express my deep regret (for what has happened).
6 I'm nowhere near as clever or as talented as our next guest on the show.

B3 Possible answers:
1 Before becoming an actress, she wanted to be a singer. After leaving Drama School, she worked in the theatre for some years. While playing 'Juliet' on the London stage, she was discovered by a Hollywood producer. Since meeting that producer, she has made ten films and won dozens of awards.
2 Before coming to this company, Mr Smith worked as a teacher in a language school. While working there, he learned a lot about people. Since coming to work here, he has had a number of positions in the company. After working here for 40 years, he became assistant manager five years ago.

UNIT 10 What are the pros and cons?

A1 2 C; 3 C; 4 D; 5 A

A2 1 In 1979.
2 In March 1986, or 7 years after they had started producing oil at Wytch Farm.
3 (The major problem was) how to transport the oil away from the oilfield. The options were: **a** by rail, or **b** by pipeline to one of three possible terminals.
4 No, there was wide consultation and a public enquiry. In fact, permission was finally given by the Secretary of State for Energy.
5 So as to avoid, as far as possible, residential areas, ecologically sensitive areas, listed buildings and ancient monuments.

A3 1 **a** is a short newspaper article; **b** is a letter to a newspaper.
2 In **a** the Council thought the pipeline was best: the writer of the letter **b** thought rail transport was best.

B1 Possible combinations:
1 Many people agree that no animals should be kept in captivity, *but* it may be the only way to help some species to survive.
2 *While* all wild animals are obviously happier living free, *nevertheless* certain forms of captivity can still give them some freedom.
3 *On the one hand* (it is true that) there are many old-fashioned zoos which were built in the 19th century and which are worse than many human prisons, *but on the other (hand)* there are many new 'wildlife parks' which try to recreate the animals' natural environment.
4 *Although* animals breed best 'in the wild' or in their own natural habitat, *unfortunately* it is becoming very difficult for some of them because Man has changed or is changing their environment in so many different ways.

UNIT 11 Could you tell me about it?

A2 1 New Zealand; 2 Canada; 3 Canada; 4 Canada; 5 New Zealand; 6 Canada; 7 New Zealand; 8 Canada

A3 1 A; 2 C; 3 D

B1 The first letter is much more informal than the second.

B2 1 Informal–Formal   5 Informal–Formal
2 Informal–Formal   6 Formal–Informal
3 Formal–Informal   7 Informal–Formal
4 Formal–Informal   8 Informal–Formal

B3 Possible sentences:
1 What I would really like to know is how much the courses cost.
2 What I am really interested in is how many students there are in a class.
3 What I did not (quite) understand was whether the recreational activities are included in the price.
4 What I would (really) like you to explain is why you only run six-week courses.
5 What I would really like to know is how you choose your families.
6 What I am really interested in is what examinations can be taken.

7 What I did not (quite) understand was how you arrange sponsorship.
8 What I would (really) like you to explain is how many specialist options one can choose.

UNIT 12 What did you do next?

A4 1 D; 2 B; 3 D; 4 A; 5 A; 6 C

B1 Story 1: Road accident situation
About six months ago I was invited to visit some friends in the country. I was looking forward to it, so I set out early. From then on, everything went wrong.
For a start, I had just turned into the main road when I crashed into another car. Just as I was reversing, a cyclist came along and rode into the side of the car.
As if that wasn't enough, as I got/was getting out of the car, a motorcyclist ran into my car door. And finally, to cap it all, I had no sooner started to cross the road to help the cyclist than a taxi knocked me down.
I did not move again much until they had taken my leg out of plaster.
While I was lying in hospital, I promised myself I would sell my car as soon as possible.

Story 2: Eventful babysitting situation
A couple of years ago I was asked to babysit for some friends of my parents. They were putting the children to bed when I arrived, so I was quite happy. But from then on, everything went wrong.
For a start, I had just turned on the TV when the five-year-old woke up. Just as I was telling her a short story, the baby woke up and started crying.
As if that wasn't enough, as soon as I picked her up, the six-year-old got up and went to the bathroom. She spilt shampoo all over the floor. And then to cap it all, I had no sooner cleaned the bathroom than the baby wanted to be changed.
They did not go back to sleep until the film on TV had finished.
While I was sitting on the bus on the way home, I promised myself I would never go out babysitting again.

B2 1 The artist said (that) he thought the picture was going very well.
2 The officer told the painter (that) there was some detergent in the kitchen.
3 The painter said (that) he would soon get rid of the stain.
4 The artist asked if/whether he could wash his hands.
5 He asked the Field Marshal where the cloakroom was.
6 The officer asked the artist if he knew how much the carpet had cost.
7 The painter told the Field Marshal (that) he was sorry about what had happened.
8 He said (that) he was sure things would go better the next day.
9 The artist asked the Field Marshal if he could/should hand him his baton.
10 He said (that) he was looking forward very much to seeing the final result.

UNIT 13 What do they look like?

A2 Valentin and Father Brown are not described.

A3 1 The Duchess of Mont St Michel and both her daughters; 2 O'Brien; 3 O'Brien and Lady Galloway; 4 Dr Simon; 5 O'Brien; 6 O'Brien; 7 Lady Margaret Graham; 8 Lord Galloway.

A4 1 True; 2 False; 3 False; 4 False; 5 True; 6 False; 7 False; 8 False

B4 Possible combinations:
1 *As well as* being extremely handsome, he (*also*) had great charm.
2 *Although* she was somewhat plump, she was an extremely graceful dancer.
3 *Despite* being still in his twenties, he was nearly bald.
4 *In addition to* having slightly cruel eyes, he also has a rather mean mouth.
5 He is quite good-looking *and* reasonably charming.
6 *In spite of the fact that* she is Scandinavian, she is surprisingly dark-skinned.
7 *Although* he must be at least fifty years old, he is still very athletic.
8 *Despite* being fairly well built, he is pretty weak physically.

UNIT 14 How can I help you?

A1 2 A; 3 B; 4 B; 5 A

A3 1 B; 2 C; 3 B; 4 D

B1 1 Instructions and advice: someone is giving a cookery demonstration.
2 Instructions and advice: someone is talking about planting seeds.
3 Advice and warning: someone is talking about plastering a wall.
4 A warning: someone is talking about using paste, acid or some other substance.
5 Instructions and advice: someone is coaching a tennis-player.
6 Advice and warning: someone is talking about using a sharp knife, saw or other tool.

B2 1 To prepare vegetables: First wash the vegetables carefully in cold water. If I were you, I'd cut them up into quite small pieces. Whatever you do, don't overcook them, otherwise they'll taste horrible.

2 To plant flowers: Don't plant the flowers until you've dug out all the weeds. It might be an idea to water the ground before you plant them. Never plant when the temperature is below zero, or else the plants will die.

3 To push-start a car: Make sure you take the handbrake off first, and then put the car into second gear. If I were you, I'd get two strong people to help. Take care not to try to start the engine until the car is moving easily, otherwise it won't start.

4 To write a composition: You should make a plan and some notes first. Then it might be an idea to decide

UNITS 12-14

... go in each paragraph. Whatever you ... you check what you have written; if ..., you could make a lot of simple mistakes.

B3 1 Don't do the second part until you have done the first part./Only do the second part when/after you have done the first part.
2 Don't sign the letter until you have read it./Only sign the letter when/after you have read it.
3 Don't turn off the gas until the water has boiled./Only turn off the gas when/after the water has boiled.
4 Don't turn off the record player until the record has finished./Only turn off the record player when/after the record has finished.
5 Don't paint a second coat until the first coat is dry/has dried./Only paint a second coat when/after the first coat is dry/has dried.
6 Don't start the composition until you have made a plan./Only start the composition when/after you have made a plan.
7 Don't write an answer until you have read the question carefully./Only write an answer when/after you have read the question carefully.
8 Don't buy the ring until she has agreed to marry you./Only buy the ring when/after she has agreed to marry you.

UNIT 15 What's the solution?

A1 The article is going to be about the dangers children face on British roads.

A3 More and more children are being killed and injured on the roads and the standard of driving is still poor. Suggested solutions include making roads narrower, using sleeping policemen, having better training for drivers and a stricter driving test.

A4 1 True; 2 False; 3 False; 4 False

A5 2 C; 3 D; 4 A; 5 C

B2 1 Yes, what we need are a number of different lunchtime 'sittings'.
2 I agree. The most sensible solution (to the problem) would be for someone from each department to fetch their post from the Post Room.
3 Yes, one answer may be for each office to have its own thermostat so that they can regulate the heating.
4 I agree. What we need to do is (to) impose a speed limit outside the factory.
5 The first priority is to find out what is making people feel ill.

UNIT 16 What can you do about it?

A1 2 D; 3 C; 4 A; 5 C

A4 1 C; 2 A; 3 B; 4 D

B Some possible sentences:
I was extremely annoyed to discover that the hotel was still being built.
To my amazement, the hotel refused to accept my credit card.
Imagine how annoyed I was when I had to change room for the third time.
The problem was this: the camp site manager had let our reserved caravan to another family.
I would appreciate it if you would deal with this matter as soon as possible.

UNIT 17 What did you use to do?

A2 Yes, the writer has fond memories of Christmas past.

A3 1 B; 2 B; 3 D; 4 B; 5 A; 6 C

B2 1 My mother *was hoping and praying* that the turkey *would taste* all right. It *was* the first year that grandmother *had allowed* her to cook it. She *did not know* that one of the children *had come* into the kitchen while she *was not looking* and *(had) poured* a packet of salt onto it. Perhaps she *should have tasted* it before she *served* it, but she *didn't*. If she *had*, the whole embarrassing episode *would not have taken* place. When we *took* our first mouthful, there *was* a chorus of splutters. My mother *had* a red face for the rest of the day.
2 I *was hoping and praying* that he *would be* at home. I *thought* he *would be* so pleased to see me. Perhaps I *should have phoned* him to let him know I *was coming*, but I *didn't*. If I *had*, the whole embarrassing episode *would not have taken* place. When I *arrived*, I *found* him dancing with another girl. As soon as I *saw* what *was happening*, I *burst* into tears and *told* him that I *would never speak* to him again!

UNIT 18 What's your own opinion?

A2 1 A; 2 B; 3 C; 4 B; 5 D

B1 Possible sentences:
1 Many people seem to feel that boarding schools have a bad effect on children, but in my experience they are good for them.
2 Some people would argue that doctors just supply drugs, but as far as I am concerned they are as important as ever in society.
3 Many people believe that boxing is an exciting sport, but my own feeling is that it should be banned.
4 No one would deny that television should entertain, but it is a fact that it should also educate and inform.
5 Many would argue that zoos are wonderful places, but as I see it they are degrading for animals.

B2 Possible beginnings:
1 At first sight, space travel seems to be a waste of money. In actual fact, however, ...
2 In theory, communism appears to be the perfect system. However, in practice, ...
3 To a certain extent it's true that America is the land of opportunity. On the other hand ....
4 Up to a point the saying 'Life begins at forty' may be

true, but . . ..
5 In some ways I agree with people who say that most pop music could be written and played by chimpanzees. However, ...
6 On the face of it, it may be true that international sport brings countries closer together, but overall I personally feel that . . ..

UNIT 19 *How to tackle Paper 1 Reading Comprehension*

General instructions
1 All of them.
2 On the separate answer sheet.
3 Before.
4 Your name and examination index number.
5 No.
6 The total score will be the number of correct answers you give.

UNIT 20 *How to tackle Paper 2 Composition*

Exam guidance for the whole Paper
1 Two.
2 One hour and 30 minutes./1½ hours./90 minutes.
3 This is just a rough guide to make sure you use the time allowed sensibly:
  a 5–10 minutes (careful reading, thinking and choosing);
  b 5–10 minutes;
  c 25–30 minutes;
  d 5 minutes;
  – then the same for the second composition.
4 No.
5 c – a combination of those that interest you and which you can write best in English.

UNITS 19-20